55

D0409131

DATE DUE

SARAH LAUGHED

SARAH

LAUGHED

* *

MODERN LESSONS

FROM THE WISDOM &

STORIES OF BIBLICAL WOMEN

VANESSA L. OCHS, Ph.D.

McGraw-Hill

New York   Chicago   San Francisco   Lisbon   London   Madrid   Mexico City
Milan   New Delhi   San Juan   Seoul   Singapore   Sydney   Toronto

*The **McGraw·Hill** Companies*

Library of Congress Cataloging-in-Publication Data

Ochs, Vanessa L.
    Sarah laughed : Modern lessons from the wisdom and stories of biblical women /
Vanessa L. Ochs.
        p.   cm.
    ISBN 0-07-140290-X
    1. Sarah (biblical matriarch).   2. Bible stories, English—O.T.—Genesis.   I. Title.

BS580.S25O25   2004
221.9'22'082—dc22   2004005352

1 2 3 4 5 6 7 8 9 0   AGM/AGM   3 2 1 0 9 8 7 6 5 4

ISBN 0-07-140290-X

Interior design by Hespenheide Design

McGraw-Hill books are available at special quantity discounts to use as premiums and sales promotions, or for use in corporate training programs. For more information, please write to the Director of Special Sales, Professional Publishing, McGraw-Hill, Two Penn Plaza, New York, NY 10121-2298. Or contact your local bookstore.

This book is printed on acid-free paper.

For Elizabeth, Dede, Rachel, Lizzie, Theresa, and Elisheva

CONTENTS

INTRODUCTION

If we go hunting in the Bible for the stories of women's lives, we will have to search very carefully. The stories told about our biblical foremothers are brief and elliptical. Sarah laughed. Rebecca drew water from the well. Rachel wept. There is little to go on. The women in the Bible live, so often, between the lines. They do not jump off the page. Should you choose to sit down and read the Bible looking for female inspiration, you might find the search frustrating.

I, too, have found it difficult to engage myself with the women of the Bible. I wish it were otherwise, because I know that ancient stories have the power to transform us. But for so long, biblical women were neither my role models nor my sources of inspiration. Not Sarah, not Rebecca, not Rachel, not my namesake, Leah (which is my Hebrew name), none of them. There was no magnetism pulling me toward their stories.

How constrained the biblical matriarchs seemed by the narrowness of their aspirations. Many—granted, not all—spent their days pining for children. Once they did have children, by and large, the women seemed to ignore or exacerbate the dysfunction of their families. If the matriarchs were role models, they were often models of whom I did not want to be.

Growing up, the biblical desert beauties who balanced clay pitchers of water on their shoulders reminded me of another problematic set of women: the annoyingly successful girls featured in that bible of adolescence, *Seventeen* magazine. They, too, knew the tips and moves that allegedly made men pay attention; they could feign fragility and sub-missiveness and rely on "female intuition" when regular thinking failed them.

I received my share of various "Great Women of the Bible" books given to girls as Sunday-school prizes for being good, helpful, prompt, and attentive. After a quick examination, I would shelve them (I preferred Nancy Drew, who could jump into her roadster and do neat stuff). These preachy, "Great Women" books didn't really want me to be great. I knew that the truly great, male or female, had to take risks and break boundaries. These books had a conservative agenda: to mold me into a pious, compliant transmitter of the values of my culture, to preserve my being a nice girl. They would have me wait for the right man to notice me and then wait for God to hear my heartfelt prayers for children, my ultimate fulfillment.

I was hardly awake to feminism, then in its nascent bra-burning stages, but I could tell there were role models out there more interesting than those Bible ladies. Only one thing I learned from the retold stories of the Bible women sparked my interest: a woman who wanted to get ahead or make a difference had to sleep, literally or figuratively, with a man who had influence. If this was true, I tried to believe it wasn't.

I had hoped that when, as an adult, I encountered women's stories through the body of ancient rabbinic legends called midrash, which tease out the stories of the Bible so that people might better connect to them, I might find my way in. But the retellings of the male sages that have been preserved through the generations, however creative and pious their efforts, have rarely helped the women of the Bible jump off the pages and into my life. Rather, the inventive additions tend to affirm a woman's otherness, as well as many of the stereotypes of women's limited social and spiritual role, that have been passed on from one generation to another. Amplified by the rabbis' explications, the women of the Bible who are gutsy (such as Dina) are often presented as being naughty; those who are bold leaders (such as Miriam) often get vilified for taking initiative and speaking out of turn.

While the ancient retellings may have enhanced the rabbis' understanding of the biblical stories and may have helped the people of their time to find the stories relevant, they help me primarily in gaining insight into the mind-set and values of the rabbis whose retellings have been passed down. My questions and concerns go unanswered. My spirit is infrequently raised.

In recent years, as a result of numerous women becoming more deeply learned in the Bible and its traditional commentaries, two new literatures *by* women and *about* women in the Bible have emerged, and they reflect a range of women's sensibilities. Both are new forms of midrash, and they aim to honor the women in the Bible and connect contemporary women to their stories.

The writers of the more conservative variety tend to beacon readers to see the women as spiritual resources. They aim to demonstrate that the matriarchs have a special relationship with God, a spirituality so innate, deep, and profound that they can see—and this is a phrase they often use—many steps into the future and anticipate what is to come. The matriarchs, seen in this light, are supposed to give women hope when there appears to be none and to help them cope with disappointments, indignities, challenges, and tragedies. Figures such as Rebecca, Tamar, or Ruth use their clairvoyance and then go a step beyond that, taking the law into their own hands. Because their ultimate goals—fulfilling the divine promise, passing along the covenant God made with Abraham, or heralding the messianic era—are so noble, how could one not admire the way they turn to subterfuge and work beneath and beyond the system? I applaud these new readings, which attribute more agency to the women of the Bible; the writers become almost like liberation theologians. But I am not especially inspired by them because the women who emerge tend to be so self-effacing, so graceful in their suffering, and too willing to put the welfare of others before their own.

The more radical new midrashim—short stories, poems, or theological essays—are being coined by women of a more liberal bent. They have been surely inspired by theologian Judith Plaskow, who has taught that feminist midrash ought to "expose the patriarchal perspective" of the ancient midrash and explore "the question it leaves open: what would happen, what is happening, as women's power begins to be freed and defined by women?"[1] I am moved by the earnest desire of these authors to give the named and unnamed women of the Bible voice, agency, and minds of their own. I applaud their efforts to see the women through the lens of their own lived experiences. Yet, I worry that in fashioning the biblical women into the figures the authors wish them to be, the women themselves get lost.

Still, I felt there had to be some way for me to connect to the women of these stories. After all, these women are my ancestors, and their sacred stories are my legacy—I couldn't just give up on them because they presented problems and challenges. I was reminded of Kathleen Norris's observation when she was drawn to the strong old women in her congregation: "Their well-worn Bibles said to me, 'There is more here than you know.'"[2] Then something happened to me that changed the way I encountered the women of the Bible and allowed them to become inspirational forces in my life.

For some months, I had been studying the story of Tamar to prepare a sermon for my prayer fellowship, a group that met each month in one of our living rooms to pray and study the chapters of the Bible designated for that week. I read both ancient and modern commentaries.

This passage from Genesis, which intrudes upon the more famous story of Joseph and his brothers, holds the essence of Tamar's story:

> *Judah took a wife for Er, his firstborn; her name was Tamar. But Er was displeasing to the Lord, and the Lord caused him to die. Judah said to Onan, "Join with your brother's wife and do your duty by her as a brother-in-law, and provide an offspring for your brother." But Onan, knowing that the seed would not count as his, let it go to waste. . . . What he did displeased the Lord, and the Lord took his life also. Then Judah said to his daughter-in-law Tamar: "Stay as a widow in your father's house until my son Shelah grows up," for he thought, "Otherwise, he will die as his brothers did." So Tamar went to live in her father's house, and many days passed.*
>
> *Tamar was told, "Your father-in-law is going to Timnah for the sheep shearing." She took off her widow's garments, covered her face with a veil, and, wrapping herself up, sat down at the entrance to Enayim, which is on the road to Timnah, for she saw that Shelah had already grown up, yet she had not been given to him as a wife.*

When Judah saw her, he believed she was a harlot, for she had covered her face. He turned aside to her by the road and said, "Come, let me sleep with you," for he did not know she was his daughter-in-law. She said, "What will you pay for sleeping with me?" He said, "I will send a kid from my flock." She said, "Only if you leave a pledge until you have sent it." He said, "What pledge shall I give you?" She said, "Your seal and your cord and the staff that you carry." He gave them to her and joined with her and she became pregnant by him. Then she went on her way. She took off her veil and again put on her widow's garments.

About three months later, Judah was told, "Your daughter-in-law Tamar has played the harlot, and what's more, she is pregnant." "Bring her out," said Judah, "and let her be burned." As she was being brought out, she sent this message to her father-in-law: "I am pregnant by the man to whom these belong." She added, "Examine these: whose seal and cord are these?" Judah recognized them and said, "She is more in the right than I, for I did not give her to my son Shelah."

—Adapted from Genesis 38:1–26

In the days of Tamar, when a man died before his wife could give birth to their first child, his brother was supposed to marry her. The child they had together would count as that of the deceased brother, and in this way, his name would carry on—a kind of reincarnation. This practice was called a levirate marriage, and it served two functions: to honor the memory of the deceased man and to provide a way for his widow to have progeny of her own and remain within his clan. Judah (one of Joseph's brothers), seeing that two of his sons had already died after being married to Tamar, feared allowing her to marry his last and youngest son. By now, Judah had concluded that Tamar was cursed—and who wouldn't? To protect his last son, Shelah, from Tamar, Judah commanded Tamar to return to her father's house and wait for Shelah to grow up. Judah had no intention of keeping his word, though he would not admit this. Perhaps he wanted to save face, to suggest he was observing the laws of levirate marriage and protecting his daughter-in-law, but this was all a pretense. Tamar was being put in cold storage.

She could not honor the memory of her deceased husbands. She could not remarry and have children with a new husband, as she was technically waiting for Judah's third son to come of age.

Tamar needed to find a way to open Judah's eyes so he might acknowledge that his actions toward her were unethical. She wanted more than his apology; she wanted him to find a way for her to have a child. From the text, one gathers there was no legal route she could have taken. She'd have to devise a plan of her own.

Thus, Tamar chose to encounter Judah at a crossroads, a place with the wonderful name "Petach Enayim," the place where eyes are opened. The interplay between revelation and disguise in Tamar's story haunted me, for the way she chose to open Judah's eyes to her pain and the injustice of his actions, and the way she succeeded in becoming pregnant, was by going undercover. Disguising her real identity, she dressed as a prostitute and slept with Judah in order to become pregnant with *his* child. Doing so allowed her to carry on her husband's name with genetic material from his family. This was the solution that Judah never would have imagined, one that protected his third son, honored the memory of his deceased sons, and addressed Tamar's needs and rights.

When Tamar's pregnancy was brought to his attention, Judah couldn't imagine that the child was, in fact, his. He wanted Tamar sentenced to death, believing she had brought shame to his family. After proving that Judah was the father of her child and that her intercourse with him was acceptable within their culture, Tamar could stand before Judah without disguises, just as she was. She led Judah to see himself and his actions for what they were. That is when Judah understood and admitted publicly that he was at fault. He exclaimed, "Tamar is right, more right than I am."

Here is the problem I had: If Tamar truly had no other choice but to sleep with her father-in-law in order to move on with her life, what kind of a lesson does that teach? That desperate, oppressed women ought to debase themselves and engage in trickery? However much Tamar's story intrigued me, I struggled with the disguise she had to endure, the degradation. While she may have "won" in the end, there was the price of that disguise. Once again, I found myself outside the biblical story.

At the time I was obsessing about Tamar's story, I had been endeavoring to find relief from a health problem that caused unrelenting pain. The constancy and duration of the pain astonished me, and after living with it for two years, my coping strategies were depleted. As my condition was invisible, I could go about my life without disclosing my struggle. I had my tricks: breathing slowly and discreetly enough through the pain or disappearing into a restroom so I could cry and then try to compose myself. The invisibility had its advantages. When I was at work, no one asked me how I was or worried about me or treated me like a sick person. At work—unlike at home, or in doctors' offices—I could pretend to be effervescent, even if that's hardly how I felt. I could feign functioning or being productive, even when my work felt shabby. I could pretend to be fully myself, and not a diminished, broken version.

Although I could not see it, the disguise was exhausting, becoming as unbearable, in its own way, as the pain itself.

One colleague knew I wasn't well. It was inevitable: we shared an office and frequently flew across the country together doing workshops on—of all things—spirituality and healing. Seeing through my disguises, he could tell when I was at my wit's end without my saying a word. He had an idea. What if I allowed him to perform an ancient healing ritual, a name-changing ceremony? Knowing I wanted to preserve my privacy, he explained I didn't even need to be there.

I had read about this ritual, though I had never seen it performed. When Jews feared someone was deathly ill or if the life of a newborn baby were endangered, a rabbi would stand before an opened Torah scroll and declare that the person of the old name was no more and was given a new or additional name. According to the tradition, the angel of death, a functionary with the ability to perform only the precise task assigned, would come seeking to carry off the person of the old name, only to find a person with a different name there instead. The angel would leave empty-handed. Having flummoxed the angel of death, the person of the new name could go on to lead a healthy life.

I shelved the idea. It seemed too magical for me, too drastic, a "big gun" I ought to save, if I were ever to use it, for a matter of life or death.

My colleague then suggested I could reclaim the ritual figuratively and still have it work. Privately, I could decide on one facet of my identity that I would give away, and in doing so, I could gain something from it. Maybe more control. Maybe some relief or liberation.

How could that help me heal? It reminded me of some contemporary healing strategies that make the ill take on so much psychic responsibility for illness that they begin to feel they are to blame. Illness had already taken away too much; I was not willing to give up a part of my identity as well. Thanking my colleague for the idea, I kept hoping an effective treatment would be found.

In the fall of the third year, I ran out of resilience. I was hospitalized and then brought to a pain clinic, where they got out their many tricks. Back home, exhausted, depressed, and only temporarily relieved of pain by a nerve block, I couldn't see marking the Jewish New Year as I usually did. Surely, I couldn't picture getting dressed up to spend the day in synagogue. I didn't even try. After my family left for the morning services, I slowly walked down to the duck pond at the foot of our road. It happened that the pond was at a crossroads: it was where the private corner of my little neighborhood intersected with the main road leading to downtown.

It is there, at that crossroads, that I encountered Tamar and she entered my story. It's where she offered up an insight from her life as a gift to me that was right for that particular moment.

If you told me something like this could happen to me, I'd have smirked. It's hard to explain what the experience is like, but it may be akin to what my Christian friends feel when they have a deep dilemma and say, "I'll have to pray on it." The voice they hear isn't their own imagination but a wellspring of divine wisdom they believe comes from outside of them. I don't mean Tamar came flying through the trees or hung over my shoulder. I mean I had sat with her story long enough beforehand and had imagined it in great detail. I had engaged it so deeply that I could be present to what Tamar would teach me when the time was ripe for her to enter my life. And the time had come.

I sat on a bench at the water's edge with my holiday prayer book, thinking that I could recite some of the day's liturgy on my own and then go back home. I am sure there were signs of the turn to autumn in the air: an invigorating coolness, the browning of the tips of the reeds by the lake, birds in new migration patterns; but I was not attentive to the beauty of the day. Swamped by pain, I couldn't focus on the text I had brought. I closed my book. I couldn't even focus enough to pray for what I wanted, which was, at this point, enough relief so that I could maintain courage to go on.

Then ten geese started swimming across the pond toward me in a V-shape. They caught my attention because they reminded me of the ten men my colleague would have had to muster up if he were to have performed the name-changing ceremony on my behalf. A curious idea came into my head: What if I imagined these geese as my own prayer quorum? I would have the beginnings of my own truly quirky and most private name-changing ceremony, wouldn't I? Tamar, I reflected, would have understood this imagined subversion of a traditional practice.

That's when I heard the voice of Tamar, and what I understood her to be telling me was this: I was standing at my own crossroads here, and if I could only open my eyes, I would see that the time had come to stop disguising myself. It might not relieve the physical pain, but it would be one less drain on my energy. With Tamar opening my eyes, I understood what my colleague at work had been getting at when he challenged me to jettison an unwanted, problematic identity and embrace one that would be more life-giving. He had been speaking in the voice of Tamar, but I wasn't yet ready to hear it.

Now I heard Tamar clearly: disguises may work, but only for so long, and they come with a price. By disguising herself as a prostitute, Tamar was indeed able to get pregnant with the child she deserved. But this strategy almost caused her death. She saved herself by taking off her disguise, revealing her true self, and obliging Judah to see her as she truly was.

I knew immediately which identity I could willingly give up. I would stop being the woman who pretended she was perfectly fine and fully functioning. I would stop defining myself by my public face, my disguise. After the holidays, I let the people at work know just how ill I had been. The details were still private, but the fact of my condition, and its implications, were not.

Once I had come out of the closet, so to speak, my phone didn't stop ringing with calls from well-wishers. I felt so moved by all the care, love, prayers, flowers, casseroles, and offers of support. People suggested concrete ways to make my work easier and take off some pressure. At that moment I grasped what Tamar wanted me to understand: it was less stressful to have some personal details of my life known than to disguise them. I may have lost some privacy, but I gained something more valuable. I discovered that the love and respect of my peers was not contingent upon my being unflappable and performing well. If this was true at work, how much more true it was at home with my family. Perhaps this new revelation should have been obvious to me, but it wasn't.

Yom Kippur, the Day of Atonement, came soon after, and I felt up to attending part of the services. Months ago, I had agreed to be called up to the Torah on this morning to recite a blessing and then chant passages from the Prophets. When the time came, I asked the visiting cantor to call me up by the name I whispered to him. It was a combination of my given Jewish name and the new name that I was about to take on. This wasn't how a name-changing ceremony would usually be performed, as there is a special formulaic incantation that is traditionally uttered, but I needed some ritual to mark that I was no longer the old person who disguised herself. I had become someone new. This public, but still private, ritual worked for me.

I had no doubts about what new name I would add to my own: Tamar.

"Arise," the cantor announced, calling me by my new name. From the back of the synagogue, my husband, who knew what I was up to and celebrated my decision, winked his support. With my new identity conferred upon me, with Tamar's passion for honesty and attentiveness to the price of disguises now laced into my soul, I recited my blessing and chanted. I started to return to my seat, and I noticed that the pain in my body was still there. I confess: for a small, unguarded, magical-thinking moment, I had allowed myself to fantasize that it might disappear altogether. Still, in the long walk down the aisle, I discovered that for the first time in months, I could focus on things with less distraction. I observed my environment with gusto, seeing the familiar with the kind of clarity one has only briefly when returning home after a long time away. I saw Naomi's newborn baby daughter. I saw Charlotte's over-the-top feathered hat. I saw my friends in the choir in their poorly fitting polyester white robes, which made them look like high school graduates. Being able to focus was a little like ecstasy, and for the first time in months, I had hope that I might pull through and mend. (In another year, which still felt like forever, I did.)

Tamar came to me as a role model and spoke deeply to me when I stopped trying to enter into her story and started letting her into mine. I discovered I could invite the other women of the Bible in as well. To allow them to enter, I'd have to sit long and quietly. As the woman who awaits her lover in Song of Songs says repeatedly, "Do not wake or rouse love until it please." I knew I had to be patient. In the meantime, I continued to study hard, immersing myself in the biblical texts, the ancient and contemporary midrashim, and the mountains of feminist biblical scholarship that have happily emerged.

Mostly I tried to listen, and what I heard just as often took me by surprise. I knew the pitfall: that you could strain so hard to listen that you started, inadvertently, to invent. I hope I have not been fooled and that the stories, teachings, and rituals that I have coined to help me better embrace and remember what I have gleaned from my encounters will encourage you to invite the women of the Bible into your own life.

What you will find in this book are stories I've written about the biblical women who have encountered and inspired me. I'd call my stories midrash, if not for the fact that the early authors of midrash claimed that their work was divinely inspired and represented the true explanations of what the Bible really meant. I make no such claims about my own stories—so I shall describe them as midrash-like.

Midrash, as I noted before, is an established rabbinic manner of interpreting the Bible by creating stories that fill in the gaps in the text and answer some of the questions that a cryptic, enigmatic, or troubling text poses. Since the second century, scholars have been composing, repeating, and then eventually writing and printing midrash, this body of work that has put flesh on the bones of the sacred work. Midrash as an art form is vitally alive today. New midrash is still being written, as readers and scholars continue to study, question, and draw inspiration from the Bible. New midrash emerges as theater, music, poetry, painting, and sculpture. Judith Plaskow describes it well: "The open-ended process of writing midrash, simultaneously serious and playful, imaginative and metaphoric, has easily lent itself to feminist use. While feminist midrash—like all midrash—is a reflection of contemporary beliefs and experiences, its root conviction is utterly traditional. It stands on the rabbinic insistence that the Bible can be made to speak to the present day."[3]

For each of the women whose story is told in *Sarah Laughed*, I have written a new midrash-like story of my own imagining that enters into the biblical story and enriches our understanding of the biblical figure. In this way, we can connect to her story in new ways and consider what insights she has for women today. The chapters are arranged in thematic sections, focusing on topics that link the biblical women to themes that are particularly pressing in our own lives: being wise, living in a woman's body, being a friend, being a parent, healing, and being in the divine presence.

Each chapter begins with a brief passage adapted from the Bible in which the woman appears. The translations from the Hebrew are (with one exception) my own, but they have surely been influenced by the excellent translation of the Jewish Publication Society. This is followed by my own retelling of the woman's story. In the third section of each chapter, I explain how that woman's story can illuminate the lives of contemporary women. I suggest what we can learn when we consult with our ancient community of sisters and how we may be empowered by the experiences and lessons of these ancient and yet still vividly available women.

Finally, because I believe that in order to really know something, we have to experience it deeply in concrete ways, each chapter closes with a ritual meant to help us remember the lessons of *Sarah Laughed* and apply them to our lives. While you can follow the ritual as a script, I encourage you to be inspired by my ritual to create a practice that resonates with your own life and spiritual commitments. It can be as simple as a recitation or as complex as a ceremony. As the great anthropologist Barbara Myerhoff said in her book *Number Our Days*, "We perform in rituals, and doing becomes believing."

PART I

BEING WISE

CHAPTER 1

EVE
TASTING WISDOM

The Biblical Story

The Holy One planted a garden in the paradise of Eden and placed in it the human who had been formed. The Holy One caused every tree to grow there: trees that were beautiful, trees yielding the most delicious fruit. The tree of life grew in the middle of the garden, and the tree of knowledge of good and bad . . . Man was to work and guard the Garden of Eden. The Holy One commanded him, "You may eat from every tree of the garden. But do not eat from the tree of knowledge of good and bad, for the moment you do, you will die."

Now God said, "It is not good for the human to be alone, so I will make him a helper. . . . She shall be called woman." . . .

Now the serpent said to the woman, "Did God really tell you not to eat the fruit of any tree in the garden?" The woman responded, "We may eat the fruit of the trees. We are forbidden to eat only the fruit of that tree in the middle of the garden—God said, 'Eat it or touch it and you will die.'" The serpent told the woman: "You will not die. God knows that when you eat from that tree, your eyes will open and you will have divine wisdom, knowing good and bad."

Seeing the delicious fruit of the beautiful tree, seeing what a desirable source of wisdom it was, the woman took its fruit and ate it. She gave some to her husband, and he ate it. Then both their eyes opened.

—Adapted from Genesis 2–3

Wisdom has built her house of seven pillars. . . . She has prepared a feast, mixed the wine, and also set the table. She has sent her women friends out to the highest places in the town to announce, "Come eat my food and drink my wine. . . . Live, walk in ways of understanding. . . . Knowledge of the Holy One is understanding. . . . If you are wise, you are wise for yourself."

—Adapted from Proverbs 9:1–6, 10, 12

Eve's Own Story

The distance from pulling a fruit from the tree of knowledge to becoming a wise woman was a short one for Eve. Or that's how it looked to Adam and her sons, who told and retold the story about Eve and the fruit that brought her wisdom overnight. Unlike Eve, they didn't notice all the steps in between, all that process. For the others, it was as if Eve had been born wise; that's who she was. She was the one you turned to because she just knew. She could figure out where you could find a misplaced tool (she'd start by asking, "Where did you see it last?" an approach no one had yet considered). She understood mysteries of the heart and could explain how you could love and hate the same person all at once.

But Eve remembered those days back when they were still in Eden, and of this she was certain: the journey toward becoming wise was hardly an overnight matter. "It's the story of my whole life," she'd say to herself and laugh. She could feel her own story continuing to unfold each day, and where it was going still remained altogether wide open. The surprise and mystery delighted her, once she got used to living well with uncertainty, to having hunches and finding out what was what over time.

When she was first becoming wise, and this was way back, even before the incident in Eden with the fruit, Eve grasped what it meant to have perspective. Literally. She started rethinking the space in Eden where she lived, experimenting with different vantage points. She would crouch low on the dirt, and seeing the expanse above, she could see she was but a wonderfully small speck in a picture of sun, moon, and stars—a whole heaven so large she could hardly fathom it. And she would climb up high in a tree and look down, and everything that was familiar to her—her shawl, her rake, her chicken, her spot of herbs—looked so small, without detail. But she could see that this was the big picture of her life. She stood on the edge of her so-perfect garden, looking out onto all that was outside and all that was unknown, and she knew this: while her familiar world was safe and predictable, there was a mysterious yet possibly wonderful world out there that would astonish, challenge, and teach her. There were boundaries she would want to preserve, she knew, but there were also boundaries she would choose to breach. With those breaches, there might be costs worth paying. There was home, and that was familiar, but if she could quiet her fear of the unknown, she could expand beyond home, venturing outward and creating new homes, new safe havens.

Shortly after leaving Eden, when the pace of learning seemed especially intense, Eve and Adam built a little house. First they lived by themselves; then the house sheltered them and their sons. Eve and Adam trusted their instincts for creation, perhaps as God did, getting some things right the first time, improvising when necessary, and making mistakes (some to be learned from and others to be laughed about) along the way. Eve trained bean vines and clusters of jasmine to climb up and over the house (a success, aesthetically speaking), but soon the house began to tilt from the weight of the foliage (some problems, she learned, were more pleasant to live with than to fix).

The first thing Eve fashioned for the inside of the house was a table made of stones. Then she went about preparing a simple feast each day, with the fruits and vegetables that they learned to harvest predictably, and the bread of their wheat and wine of their vines that she learned to make. (Yes, the wine came about when the grape juice stayed out too long. This was yet another mistake that seemed better to enjoy than to correct.)

"Come eat at my table," she would announce to the others, and they kept returning each day, morning, noon, and night, as if it were a ceremony they had been performing their whole lives. As the family ate

Eve's food, Eve fed them bits of what she was learning, trying it out on them. Because what did she really know for sure? At the beginning, it was all just inklings, speculations, and hypotheses, not the kind of knowing you have in your bones and trust with every inch of your being—that would come long, long down the line. Sitting at Eve's table, her family was richly nourished. How did she perform this transformation upon them? Mostly, she led them to feel whole, loved, and safe. And because of this, they were always eager to return, hungry to eat and learn.

In the process of becoming wise, Eve acquired the knack for circumspection. She started to mark her words, to take the implications of her thoughts seriously, to realize they mattered and were worth remembering. She noticed how often she talked silently to herself inside her own head, making up stories that made sense of her day, stories that held her together. She found herself sharing these stories aloud, over and again, with the others, and doing that made her feel less alone and more connected. She learned that some of her thoughts, when shared, could be hurtful. She came to understand the power of holding her tongue. She saw, too, that her loving words—even a touch or a glance—could heal, and she saw that words of rebuke could cause the color to drain from someone's face. She saw that her attentive silence provided the invitation for others to speak to her in confidence.

As Eve continued to grow, somewhere along the line, she noticed God. Precisely where and how that happened was hard for her to say. For Adam and the boys, who did not yet understand the concept of process, Eve's getting God, like everything else, seemed a sudden and curious thing, coming with the fruit incident. Eve knew differently. Sensing God and grasping the idea of God's presence came as sparks of insight, some intense and some glimmers, along the way. She would lie next to Adam as she first awoke, raising her arm upward and suspending it there, and wondering: "Is it my desire that allows me to move my arm or keep it still, or is there a force greater than myself, propelling the motion?" God came to Eve as a good many moment-to-moment feelings about the sacredness of all this, a pervasive sense that she would always feel wonder. God came to Eve when Adam touched her on her shoulder and said, "Eve, I think you look sad." This gesture of kindness felt much larger than a gift that came from Adam alone. And then there was the way Adam could sometimes see inside her when she said nothing at all.

God came to Eve without flashes of light, apparitions, visions, angels in the guise of visitors; there were no talking animals, no overturnings of the predictable ways of nature. There was just a lifetime of ordinary experiences, especially the messy, hard-luck times outside the garden. They coalesced and affirmed Eve's growing hunch, pointing outward toward something bigger and inward toward something deeper, holding her. She noticed how easily she could lose sight of God's presence when the connection felt fragile, and how, just as easily, she could rediscover that presence and feel it richly.

Eve made a conscious project of teaching her sons everything she knew, once she became persuaded by the hunch that she wouldn't be around to be their mother forever. She told them life wasn't fair, for one, and that brothers must keep each other whole, for two. She taught them that knowing the difference between good and bad was hardly ever a clear matter, and they would spend their lives discerning the gray areas. She knew they would have to find all this out for themselves, just as she had, but she told them just the same. They were not the best of students and didn't mask their boredom. "It's Eve stuff," they would say and touch at their hearts in a pitter-pattering way. What they meant was this: the things Eve knew could make you feel more whole, but they wouldn't necessarily help you ride a horse or prop up a tilting fig tree after a violent storm. Still she taught, and they pretended not to listen intently, lest she be too pleased and get all smug on them.

However often Eve insisted they had it all wrong, Adam and the boys persisted in telling the fruit story again and again. You had to hand it to them: it made for a good and coherent story. Eve was struck by the way the fellows failed to distinguish between knowledge as a possession that made you feel powerful, and knowledge as a stance in the world, an inquisitive approach to becoming a deep and complex human being. Maybe the idea that knowledge gave you clout and power was true to the experience of her men, but it did not feel true for Eve. For Eve, seeking wisdom was about noticing, registering, and making sense. Knowing made her distinctly more alive. She did not name that feeling power, but surely it was.

If only there were other women in her world to experience knowing as she did. What a feast Eve would make for them! They would come to her table and contribute all they knew, and each one would leave much richer than before.

Eve Speaks to Us

Eve was self-taught. She didn't have parents to teach her the way of the world. Eve's sole companion, Adam, was so much a reflection of herself. Gazing attentively and deeply into his eyes, there was little she saw in them that she didn't already know. Lacking a human teacher, she turned to God for wisdom. God, acting with compassion, knowing that with knowledge comes pain, was not keen to share. Like those parents who resist imparting all they know to their children for fear the children will be too delicate to bear all the complication and harshness, God seemed to hold back, as if imagining Eve could be protected and kept innocent. But being kept in the dark made Eve hungrier to know more and to have experiences. She found neither joy nor safety in her bewilderment. Eve knew she could never be fully human if she learned only what was safe, obvious, and permissible to know. Even if God meant well in wishing to preserve her ignorance, Eve would become a learner just the same. Surely God would come round and proudly celebrate all that persistent Eve had figured out.

Martin Buber, in his reflections on Genesis, understood that Eve saw and contemplated on multiple levels, ways sometimes distinct from Adam's. Looking at the tree in the Garden of Eden, Eve

> . . . *does not merely see that it is a delight to the eye, but also sees in it that which cannot be seen: how good its fruit tastes and that it bestows the gift of understanding. This seeing has been explained as a metaphorical expression for perceiving, but how could these qualities of the tree be perceived? It must be contemplation that is meant, but it is a strange, dreamlike contemplation. And so, sunk in contemplation, the woman plucks, eats, and hands to the man. . . . She seems moved by dream-longing.*[1]

Eve set out on her own to learn what she needed to know to become human. Without a comprehensive plan, she struck out following her hunches and intuitions, doing what Mary Catherine Bateson calls "composing a life." Bateson is referring to ways that women allow their lives to lead them down uncertain paths and permit themselves to follow their instincts and be flexible—even if it means having to reinvent themselves over and over again. Eve discovered that the facility for seeking wisdom and amassing it was hers all along. Feeling hunger, feeling love, feeling pain—each physical experience, catalogued in her body and in her mind—was part of what she knew and who she was. She needed only to reflect on her experience, to take it seriously, and to fathom it even more deeply by transmitting what she was learning to the others.

Early on, Eve discovered there would be "snakes" along her path. They were those who would stand in her way, threatening to curtail her search for wisdom by saying, "Oh, you'll never understand that; you don't have a head for it, so why waste your time?" Or "Why ever would you want to know that?" Eve discovered how easily she could be her own "snake," blocking her own path, when in moments of fading courage she'd resist examining assumptions she held, long after she suspected they didn't hold water.

When you become wise like Eve, you don't let others tell you what is safe for you to learn, try out, explore, or investigate. You don't let anyone tell you your spirit is too fragile to get knee-deep in harsh or distressing realities. You know what you need to encounter to become wise, and you venture forth. You let no one tell you what you do or do not "have a head for," because the head you need is the one you already have or can develop. You let no one tell you what kind of learning is a waste of your time or what's too serious for you, or not serious enough. You alone are the judge of what's heavy and what's lightweight. (Back in the 1970s, a woman who wanted to do graduate scholarship on women was inevitably steered by her advisors—male or female—toward a topic that was more "mainstream." She'd be told that if she wrote about women, she'd be considered lightweight and would never be taken seriously in her field. Fortunately, a good many women, many who became the founding mothers of women's studies in various disciplines, disregarded their advisors' advice. Their careers weren't easy, but they opened doors for younger women scholars who wanted to study the lives, histories, and artistic creations of women.)

To become wise like Eve, you discover ways to weave together your book learning and your life learning. A distinct time of synthesis came for me when I was eighteen, a college junior studying classical French acting in Paris. There was a gifted older student at the drama conservatory, an actor from Belgium who seemed incredibly adult to me because he already had a wife, an infant son, a night job waiting tables, a cigarette always in his hand, some laudable acting credits to his name, and a strategy for first launching his career in Paris theater, and then his wife's. "Old" Franc must have been all of twenty-seven. We met at a café near the room I rented on Avenue Niel so we could work together on a scene from a play by Racine. As I was reading my lines, which must have been about burning up from unrequited love (I knew beans about this from real life), Franc said, "Put down the script." I did as he said, which surprised me, because I've never been especially obedient—but Franc's voice seemed urgent, and maybe I intuited what he would say.

"You really think that everything you need to know about human emotions can be learned in books, don't you?"

"I do not," I said, but I suspected Franc was right. While I had loved the *idea* of acting ever since I had starred as Betsy Ross in elementary school and as Maria in *The Sound of Music* at summer camp, I never felt entirely competent on the adult stage, which demanded not just good projection, elocution, and grace (those three I could handle), but baring of my soul on stage (forget about it, impossible). Temperamentally, I was very much a "head person," adept at gathering and synthesizing information from books and keeping it at arm's length. In Paris, when I wasn't studying acting at the conservatory or going to the Comédie Française, the French national theater, I wasn't exactly tasting life. I spent my days with my nose in a book, researching the history of French theater in the Bibliothèque Nationale. When I needed a break, I'd close my books and wander around the academic bookstores or prowl the bookstands along the Seine looking for the works of the classical dramatists. I bought yogurt and bread at the market and ate alone (while reading) in my room.

"If you dared to put yourself in the bath of life," Franc continued, "you'd start feeling more comfortable in your own skin. Get your nose out of your books! Then you'll be ready to act and not just read the lines like a clever schoolgirl."

I attempted to protest. The life of the mind—scholarship (about which Franc admitted he knew little)—was *not* an escape from real life. Even though it took place in musty libraries and its exhilarations didn't leave you sweaty, couldn't scholarship still count as one way to be passionate about life? Besides, I was really good at it, good at gathering up what we thought of then as "objective" knowledge about the world, good at reading between the lines to discern multiple layers of meaning. That was what I was rewarded for in school and what I felt safe and powerful doing. But I could see that scholarship provided only a partial picture, one lens through which to experience life.

I was miffed that Franc presumed to see inside my soul! As I walked back to the nunlike room I rented and closed the door, I had to recognize that Franc had seen correctly. As far as personal experience went, all I knew about the great passions the French dramatists wrote about— romantic love, honor, and loyalty—came from books.

I traipsed around Paris in the cold December rain with an image that wouldn't leave my head. I pictured myself in my grandmother's enormous white raised bathtub with clawed lion's feet, and I saw the stuff of life floating all around me like tub toys: A loaf of bread. A refrigerator. A telephone. A shoe. A lover. A child. A house. A book.

Not in an instant, because I am pokey about making major life changes, but eventually, I came round. I would risk expanding my learning beyond books and start learning from life, preferably my own.

The cliché is that you go abroad to find yourself. I went abroad and hid in dark theaters and libraries and bookstores—safe, familiar, lonely places—because I was overwhelmed by all the unfamiliarity. While most people go to Paris to experience life more emphatically, I took Franc's advice and left Paris months before I had planned to, thinking I might have better luck getting into the bath of life if I headed home. I had met an American man just days before going to Paris and I planned to discover if I was supposed to fall in love with him. He had been writing me what were potentially love letters (His handwriting was chicken-scratchy awful, so I had to infer a lot. What might have been "How is the weather?" I chose to read as, "I can't live without you, come back."). Looking back, after having been married for thirty years, I can say getting into the bath of life with this particular American man was a good move. I have learned how to love and to be loved by him; we have learned how to sculpt a life together. (And we're both still figuring it out.) I also learned that I wasn't meant to be an actress after all, but a writer.

Eve teaches us that life gets us wise, bit by bit, and we need to notice, appreciate, and celebrate each step of the way as we carve it out for ourselves, no matter how hit-or-miss. Eve celebrates the path of getting there, however complex or convoluted. In *Women's Ways of Knowing*, a collaboration of four women authors, we learn that women "view reality and draw conclusions about truth, knowledge, and authority in distinctive ways"—including accessing understanding through shared experience, through feeling empathy, through dialogue, and through the questioning of authority and accepted truths.[2] When you become wise like Eve, you regard all ways of learning with respect.

Embracing the Gift of Eve

To mark your own birthday, the day that celebrates not only your creation but also the very first day you began to learn, affirm your Eve-like wisdom by teaching something you have learned that has deepened your world. By now, you're wise enough to know that you don't need to measure your self-worth by how many people succeed in remembering your birthday without prompting. So go ahead: Invite people you love, and new acquaintances you'd like to know better, to a little birthday feast, and transmit at least one of the "apples of wisdom" you have acquired this past year—or over your lifetime. As Lady Wisdom, you can say to your guests, "Here! Eat deeply!"

What might you do? Read from the work of an author whose writing has touched you. (Some of my favorites have been Barbara Meyerhoff, M. F. K. Fisher, Henri M. Nouwen, and Anna Halprin.) Reveal how you figured out how to put some zip back into your social life. Demonstrate a gravity-defying yoga pose you never expected you could do. Reveal your strategy for keeping your world together when hard news breaks your heart.

On my fiftieth birthday, I summoned my daughters and sister Susan to a ladies' weekend away and, over an Indian dinner, shared some things I have learned over the years that I believe are worth knowing. My first teaching was one they all knew by heart, so they said it along with me: "Movie theaters are always cold, even in the summer, so always take a sweater." My second teaching was a practice of mine they had surely observed: "When my world falls apart, I chop vegetables. Onions are especially good, because then you get to cry without having to explain what's wrong if you don't want to. Then you stir-fry the vegetables with garlic and soy sauce, cook up some rice, and by then, although your despair may still be there, at least you have something to eat! The next day, you chop, you cook, you fold laundry, and you shower and get dressed. You keep going through the actions of sustaining life until finally the day comes along when you discover that without your being aware, happiness and hope have crept back in."

Invite your guests to bring only one kind of present: an insight of their own to share! It could be a personal epiphany or wisdom they have received. It could also be a useful hint: the name of a good massage therapist or consistent hair dresser, the day the fancy European shoe store in town has its one-day-only sidewalk sale, a list of high school students who sometimes say yes when you ask them to babysit.

Serve fruit, of course. Or, make my version of my wise friend Helena's Fresh Apple Cake. (The only reason I still have the recipe on my refrigerator is that Helena not only laminated the index card she printed it on, but also affixed a magnet to the back of it. In her version there are several steps. In mine, you throw everything into a bowl at once, and it works, I think, just as well.)

2 cups peeled, diced apples
1 cup sugar
1 teaspoon vanilla
¼ cup oil

    1 cup flour
    ½ teaspoon salt
    1 teaspoon baking soda
    1 egg
    ½ cup chopped nuts (optional)

Preheat the oven to 375°F. Combine everything in a bowl. Bake in a greased 9″ square pan for 40 minutes.

CHAPTER 2

HAGAR
ENVISIONING A
POSITIVE OUTCOME

The Biblical Story

Abraham took some bread and a skin of water and gave them to Hagar. He placed them in a sack, slung it over her shoulder, and sent her and their child Ishmael away. Hagar roamed about in the wilderness of Be'er-sheva. When her bread and water were all gone, Hagar left the child under one of the bushes and went down and sat at a distance, a bowshot away. She thought: "I cannot watch as the child dies." Sitting at a distance, she wept.

God heard the cry of the boy, and an angel of God called to Hagar from heaven, saying, "What troubles you, Hagar? Do not be afraid, for God has heard the cry of the boy where he is. Come, lift up the boy and hold him by the hand, for I will make a great nation of him."

God opened Hagar's eyes and she saw a well of water. She went and filled the skin with water and let her son drink. God was with the boy as he grew up; he lived in the wilderness and became an archer. His mother found a wife for him in the land of Egypt.

—Adapted from Genesis 21:14–21

Hagar's Own Story

Hagar reached Be'ersheva unable to take another step, so hot was this wilderness, even at nightfall. There were no paths, no souls, only endless hills of sand that shifted in the warm wind. The few loaves of bread

Abraham had provided them had run out two days ago. Why had he given them food at all, knowing they would quickly starve even if they only nibbled each day? What was he sustaining her for? To endure more anger and suffering? If only she had water to drink, she could think beyond her despair and the tear in her heart. Soon they would be bones picked over by the vultures that screeched over them. The once-wild eyes of her son Ishmael were now dark and sunken. He reached his arms up to her and his eyes asked for water. There was none, Hagar knew without looking.

"Carry me?" his eyes asked, for he was feverish and short of breath. But Hagar hadn't the strength to carry him beyond a few feet.

Hagar placed Ishmael under the only bush she could spy that had no thorns. The leaves of the low, willowy branches were grey-green and soft like lamb's ears, and she nested him inside them. His breath was so shallow. If she could breathe love and more life into him she would. Surely he would perish this night. Could a mother witness this and not perish herself? "How could I have agreed to give birth to this child," she chastised herself, "seeing how he is being taken away from me like this? Forgive me, Ishmael. I have failed you." She felt such shame. She was jealous of all other mothers blessed to see their children embarking upon life. She watched him in his bower, guarding him like an angel until he hardly breathed and she could watch no more. She dragged her feet across dusty, cracked earth and sand, dropping down a short distance from her son. She leaned against a rock and prayed through her tears: "Speak to me in my dreams, Keeper of Dreams. Tell me how I can go on, how I can breathe life into my son, how I can protect him when I have nothing to give him and nothing to do for him. Send me a dream that will seal us in a new fate, a dream that will sustains us, or the wilderness shall consume us."

Hagar fell quickly asleep, the salt of her tears sealing her lashes against her eyes. She woke in the morning to the sound of Ishmael's breathing. "My imagination," she thought, "a trick of the mind or delirium, for Ishmael, so weak, could not have lasted the night." Yet here he was, rolling from side to side, pulling his knees up to his chest, his two hands folded under his cheek to make a pillow. He smiled, as if caught in a happy dream of playing with sticks and stones.

Hagar stayed very still, straining to recall the dream she had incubated. There was nothing, just an empty buzzing in her memory. There was no dream. . . . How could this happen? Had her memory abandoned her, or had God?

She tried to rise to her feet, but a wave of sleep pulled her back down to the rock, and she curved herself into it, as if she were nestled again inside her mother's womb. She woke from this second sleep into the harsh sunlight of high morning, and this time her memory was rich with the details of a morning dream.

How real it all seemed, as if it were no dream at all.

Not daring to move, lest her memory become dislodged, Hagar held on to each detailed image and watched it unfold slowly as if it were a butterfly hatching. There had been an angel, a messenger of God: a disembodied voice at first, then a calling out from the tips of palm fronds, then a moaning from the stars, then a woman enrobed in grey clouds, then a snake coiling around her arm and a fox sleeping beside her, its fur on her neck. Hagar had been in the dream too, sleeping silently against the rock. She was her younger self, a girl who had once been a princess, a very young woman who trusted the goodness of Abraham and melted into his arms, made giddy by the sisterly friendship Sarah offered, the promises she had made of being close until death. In the dream it had been Ishmael who had cried out loudly. These were not the tears of a fretful child, but wails of sadness, the keening of a man mourning for a tribe and a dream of blessings that had been devoured in the jaws of a lion. Then out of Ishmael came the voice of an adult man, "My father has abandoned me. Hear me, answer me. Hold me."

The angel disappeared to consult in the heavens. Upon returning, the angel reported, "God has heard Ishmael crying."

"I, too, hear him cry," Hagar said. "Does God hear the same cry his mother hears?"

The angel disappeared again to consult, then returned. "God knows your boy's soul."

"Then," Hagar told the angel, "God is El Ro'i, the God who sees deep inside me too."

In her dream, the boy's crying had ceased, and Ishmael stretched in his sleep, as if he were dreaming of playing with baby lambs in a pasture in spring. The angel drew a circle in the sand around Hagar and Ishmael. "Step outside the circle of your fear and aloneness, Hagar."

Hagar awoke and before she opened her eyes, she reviewed the dream God had sent her. But what did it mean? There were no dream interpreters in the wilderness; she would have to rely on herself.

Hagar opened her eyes slowly. Where was Ishmael, whose body she dreaded seeing? She heard his steps as he walked in the direction of the sun. Hagar saw his back, his feet, and the backs of his arms swinging. He was walking toward the sound of trickling water. She rose and followed him, keeping some steps behind, so as not to startle him. He was peering down into a well. He turned to his mother, sensing her presence: "We are not alone anymore."

Touching the edges of the well, Hagar moistened her hands with water and patted Ishmael's face, and then her own, washing away the salt that had crusted on her skin. She reached into the well and filled her empty skin with water, and they both drank deeply, passing the skin back and forth between them. It was but water, and still they felt full, as if they had been to a wedding feast and had celebrated with beef, yogurt, bread, and cakes made of nuts and honey. She gave a name to the well: "Well of the living one who sees me," for it was there that God saw her and gave her eyes for seeing beyond the moment.

It was finding this well that opened up the meaning of the dream, Hagar knew. From her dream, Hagar discovered she and her son could keep waking up each morning and going to sleep each night if they held on to the conviction that a new day of promise would unfold. They needed to open their eyes to see promise even when it was least apparent, and they would move toward it. In this way, they would live and God would live with them.

Hagar Speaks to Us

When Sarah and her husband, Abraham, were unable to conceive a child together, Sarah persuaded Abraham to have a child with Hagar, her Egyptian maidservant. Hagar agreed and gave birth to Ishmael, who would be considered Sarah's own child. But after Sarah and Abraham eventually and miraculously succeeded in having a child of their own, named Isaac, Sarah ordered Abraham to send Hagar and Ishmael away into the wilderness. Abraham was disturbed by Sarah's plan, but he was commanded by God to obey Sarah's wish, as it mirrored God's will.

What a harsh turn of fate for Hagar. One day she was the mother of an important son divinely ordained the father of a nation; the next day, she and her son were exiled with only some bread and water. They journeyed into a wilderness of oblivion until their resources were depleted. Hagar doubted her capacity to prevent her son from dying. She cried until she fell asleep, and had a dream.

In her dream, Hagar was assured by an angel that God was well aware of Ishmael's pain, which of course was Hagar's pain as well. God knew how intertwined the boy's tears and his mother's heartbreak were, and was moved to respond with compassion. God gave Hagar a powerful directive for the time being and an omen for the future: "Come, lift up the boy and hold him by the hand, for I will make a great nation of him."

Much wisdom is held within these words. Hagar was being told: "Although the place you stand in now may feel utterly bleak, have the courage to imagine that a time will eventually come when the crisis of the current moment is behind you. It could take time, but it will come. Even when you are challenged, if you hold onto the possibility of change, you may discover you have the resources to help it unfold."

Waking from her dream, Hagar knew she must follow the spiritual direction God had given her. Hagar allowed herself to see the well of water (*be'er*, the site's namesake, means "well") that lay before her and her son. Perhaps the well was there even before she had her dream. But Hagar was so convinced she could not save her son or lead her son into the future that she could not yet see that what they needed to survive was already within her reach. I imagine that Ishmael helped Hagar to see the well, as our children, who we think are so dependent on us, are so often our teachers and guides.

Hagar could now see that no matter how harsh their fate was at that moment, God had provided her and her son with a resource that would allow them to sustain themselves into the future. It was not just the water that God provided, but also the ability to see the range of resources that were in front of her all along: her love for her son; her resilience; her plans to raise him, find him a wife, and help him to establish himself as the head of a nation. She saw that she didn't need to be rescued. She could save them both, and as Ishmael grew, they would care for each other.

Hagar filled her skin with water and let her son drink, and he was revived. She took care of herself too. This is a hallmark of a mother who guides the way: she knows that when she cares for herself, she not only retains her capacity to parent well but also models the importance of self-preservation.

Hagar was able to help Ishmael survive beyond this crisis, even beyond the trauma of having been rejected by his father and cast out of his familiar world. Had she not assured him that he could aspire to greatness, had she not helped him achieve his goals, he might not have claimed these aspirations for himself. Hagar, the visionary, was a pathfinder as well: she had the psychic strength to imagine a new civilization into being. In fact, Hagar was the first woman in the Bible to forge a new society without the protection of a spouse, a tribe, or a community. Hagar learned just how resourceful she was: she could move from the dream of a whole new world to its realization, and she would be able to transmit that vision to her son, who would continue to build on it as her legacy.

Ishmael inherited the insight his mother acquired in her dream. She taught him to open his eyes to the resources at hand and to look positively toward the future. Having grown up in the wilderness and having learned to survive masterfully in this new place, he became an archer. He readily fashioned a bow and arrow and discovered he had the skills and instincts to hunt for the food that would feed them. Ishmael accepted the Egyptian wife his mother selected for him. Could it be that this was someone he had spied before? Perhaps his mother helped him see that the one who was to be his beloved was already right there, even when he despaired of ever meeting the right woman. Despite fraught beginnings, Ishmael went on to lead a life of great accomplishment. He became the father of twelve sons, each the head of his own tribe, and he lived a long life.

Hagar raised a son who could envision peace and reconciliation. When his father, Abraham, died, Ishmael appeared at the funeral. He had every reason not to be there: disrespect for the father who had sent both him and his mother into exile, jealousy of his younger half-brother Isaac who had usurped his place in his father's heart. Despite this, Ishmael joined Isaac as they peacefully and collaboratively buried their father at a family cave in Machpela. Today, we ourselves pray that the children of Sarah's son Isaac (the Jews) and the children of Hagar's son Ishmael (the Muslims) might, in our lifetime, dream of rising above differences, celebrating common origins, and achieving peace.

When we are challenged, Hagar, who sustained herself and her son in the worst of circumstances, can inspire us. Consider these hallmarks of Hagar's approach: She is realistic in evaluating her situation and doesn't shy away from feeling and expressing her anguish. She reaches out for help and takes the good advice she is given. She allows herself to be comforted, lifted up, and convinced of her own capabilities and resources. She learns that when you wipe the tears from your eyes and see more clearly, you can discover what you do have. In fact, the solutions you desire and the resources you need to draw on might be right there in front of you.

Hagar teaches us to trust that even in bleak times, we still have the capacity for clarity of vision and hope. Hagar tells us: "Wipe away your tears. Open your eyes. When you dream of a better future ahead, you will discover it."

This was the advice my friend Rachel once gave me, though at the time, I did not understand. I had gotten one of the worst phone calls a parent could imagine: my daughter, studying abroad, was in the hospital and was in great pain. She knew she needed immediate surgery but couldn't persuade the doctors to recognize the emergency. My husband, Peter, raced to the airport and took the first plane to England. I booked a flight for the next day. I sat in my kitchen, making phone calls to arrange for my mother to stay with my younger daughter. I felt terrified and powerless. All I could do for the time being was pray and fax medical records over to the hospital, and hard as I tried, my hands trembled too much to punch in the right phone numbers. I felt as if we were spiraling down into a dark drain. It was at this point that Rachel called, and I poured my heart out. She said that while we were in the midst of a nightmare right now, and it felt impossible to imagine a time when the nightmare would be over and behind us, she promised that we would indeed all pull through this together. Peter would make sure our daughter got the care she needed and would be there with her. I would be there soon enough to care for her, and she would recuperate. Before we knew it, we would all be back home together sitting around the dinner table, and there would be laughter and normalcy and we would be worrying about all kinds of mundane things, like finding the time to get the boxes to the recycling center or finding the right dresses for a cousin's wedding.

After three weeks, Rachel's prediction proved correct. My husband got to the hospital in time to fight for the necessary operation, and I arrived in time to be at our daughter's side as she recovered. My daughter got out of the hospital, and while she recovered, we stayed together at the picture-perfect country home of dear friends, complete with a litter of newborn Shelties. Within days, we were gathering lavender in their backyard, making dried flower arrangements, and playing with the puppies, and within weeks we were home again, sitting around the dining room table laughing. Although we were exhausted and shaken by the crisis, we did—just as my friend promised—become citizens in the land of the normal once again.

Embracing the Gift of Hagar

Hagar, as some read her story, discovered the resources with which she needed to sustain herself and her son by incubating a dream. By incubating a dream, you too can seek guidance as you look toward the future. Some who value dreams understand them as messages from God. Others see them as fonts of wisdom from our deepest selves, which we can access only with conscious effort. However you understand dreams, you can find strength and direction in them. Like the well of water before Hagar, a dream is a resource for wisdom that is right there in front of us, readily available but so easy to ignore.

Dream incubation was practiced in many ancient civilizations. Dream incubators of old would usually go to a holy site, where they would prepare by offering sacrifices or making libations. Before going to sleep, they would pose a question to God or to their powerful spirits in the hope that a response would come in a dream. In the morning, if the meaning of the dream was not apparent, they might then bring their dream to an interpreter, a ritual expert who would explicate the divine revelation.

In Hagar's dream, God's messenger told her to sustain herself and her child with the water she could find in the well and to anticipate that her son would survive and become the father of a great nation. Hagar's task was to stay directed in raising her child, to believe that she could get them beyond this crisis and continue to guide her son along the pathway to his distinguished destiny. Without a dream interpreter to rely on, Hagar found the meaning of her dream on her own.

To incubate a dream that will help you receive guidance, prepare for sleep by spending some time writing or thinking about the particular issue that concerns you. In one concise sentence, write down a question that you hope your dream might resolve and place it under your pillow. If your practice is to recite a bedtime prayer, add a request that you will receive a dream that addresses your concerns. Keep paper by your bedside so you can write down any dreams or dream fragments that you recall the moment you wake up. If you don't recall any dreams after that first night, repeat the process of requesting a dream response for a few nights, as sometimes it takes a while for a dream you are incubating to arrive and register itself in your memory.

To discern how your dream connects to the question you have posed, you will need to interpret it. While there is a long tradition of bringing incubated dreams to professional dream interpreters who tease out a dream's meaning, you can bring your dream to a trusted friend or advisor or, as Hagar did, try to interpret it yourself. Ask yourself these questions: Why do you think this particular dream came as a response to your dream question? Is there some image or character in the dream that suggests (even in an extremely symbolic way) the challenge you are experiencing? Just as Hagar's dream pointed to a well, does your dream point to some resource, material, or person already in your world that could offer direction and assistance? Is there some image or episode in your dream that could direct you toward greater hopefulness? While your dream may not offer a complete solution, like Hagar's, it can point you in the right direction. Hagar's dream led her to a well that quenched her thirst—that was only the first step, but it led to the next, and the next. She could take it from there, and you could too.

CHAPTER 3

MIRIAM
INSPIRING OTHERS

The Biblical Story

Moses stretched out his hand over the sea and God caused the sea to go back. The waters split and the Children of Israel came through the midst of the sea on dry land, the waters forming a wall for them on their right and on their left. Then God said to Moses, "Stretch your hand over the sea and the waters will return upon Egypt." The waters returned, covering the chariots and riders of Pharaoh's army that had followed after them into the sea. That day, God delivered the Children of Israel from the Egyptians.

Having witnessed God's wondrous and awesome power, the Children of Israel trusted God. Moses and the Children of Israel sang this song to God, uttering these words: "I will sing to the Lord who has triumphed gloriously; the horses and drivers have been hurled into the sea."

Then Miriam the prophetess held a timbrel in her hand, and all the women followed her, dancing with their own timbrels. Miriam chanted for them: "I will sing to the Lord who has triumphed gloriously; the horses and drivers have been hurled into the sea."

—Adapted from Exodus 14–15

Miriam's Own Story

She had crossed the sea. Reaching the shore, she was drenched and breathless. "God took me out of Egypt," Miriam said aloud, knowing she needed to form the words in her mouth and hear them to affirm that what she had experienced was not just a dream. "We were slaves; and now we are free." Before stopping to rest, before pausing to begin to absorb the shock of their miraculous rescue, Miriam put down the pack she had strapped on her shoulders and took out the timbrel she had carried with her out of Egypt, and inspected it. Though it had gotten damp, the goat skin had remained taut and the small bells she had wound around the wooden frame years ago still rang clearly. With each step she had taken toward freedom, she had heard the bells jangling softly in her pack. They served as accompaniment to the voice of assurance Miriam heard:

You will be safe.
You will be free.
You will have a home.
You will celebrate.
You will never forget.
You will be grateful always.
You will live each day in holiness.

With this voice in her ears, she had been lifted up through the perilous crossing, lifted above her own fears. The words carried her with hope, even as the waves roared horribly as they were swept upward and made to part, creating for her people a safe pathway guarded with walls of water.

This was how it had been before, even when she was a child: Miriam hearing what others could not, Miriam trusting the voice of assurance. She knew she could hold on to hope when reason might lead others to despair. Women had come to think of Miriam as their leader, and they believed the future she envisioned would come to pass. They called her "Miriam the prophetess," first bestowing this name when, as a young midwife, she inspired the Hebrew women to resist despairing over

Pharaoh's darkest decree: the killing of Hebrew sons. "Act against logic," she told them. "Go ahead, fall in love, make babies, and imagine you will watch them grow up and have rich lives."

Miriam shook the water from her timbrel and blotted it dry across the front of her robes. She saw now that the timbrel's ribbons were stuck together. How frayed they were, the same ones she had attached as a child. Back then the timbrel was just a plaything that came out whenever she invented pretend celebrations, for their lives, as the children of slaves, were too bleak for real celebrations. As she now untangled the ribbons between her fingers, she composed the words she would sing for the women.

She made her way a bit farther inland until she could walk without her feet getting stuck in the moist sand. Miriam began to dance alone. She took gliding steps from side to side, and then she spun, her wet scarves spiraling around her neck and waist and clinging to her. Soon the Hebrew women, who had been right behind her, reached this same patch of dry land. There were mothers carrying heavy toddlers too tired to walk, granddaughters supporting the elderly. The first image they beheld as free women was Miriam dancing. They watched as she held her timbrel to her heart, reached it up to the heavens, and then stretched it outward to welcome this people streaming out from the turquoise sea that had grown quiet.

Following Miriam's lead, as if she had given them precise instructions, the women resisted the natural impulse to collapse and cry. Instead, they reached into their packs or baskets for their own timbrels and blotted them dry. First girls danced with Miriam, snaking behind her, picking up the quality of her movement. Then one by one, women— the young and the old—did their best to follow Miriam's simple steps, until they were all dancing and their timbrels were reaching out in all directions. Even the frail and the elderly rocked back and forth or just danced along with their eyes. Babies inside their mother's wombs sang and danced too, for the wombs had grown transparent as glass and the babies saw God's presence. The sound of bells and drums grew as loud as the waves of the sea had been and muffled their still-resounding memory of the shrieking soldiers who had pursued them.

Though the women had trusted Miriam implicitly before, they had raised their eyes with doubt when, in their last moments, as they rushed to pack the absolute essentials before leaving Egypt, Miriam had gone from house to house offering calm instruction: "Pack your timbrel, because we will soon be dancing together in freedom."

"A timbrel?" they asked. "Pack a timbrel when we are struggling to fit the memories and trappings of a lifetime into one basket? A timbrel in place of an extra water jug?"

Had anyone else instructed them to pack timbrels, they would have ignored her. But Miriam could push others toward her enticing vision. She could lead them to consider the sparkling possibilities she embraced, no matter how outlandish. She painted a picture of the rich and holy culture they would build together, one their great-grandchildren would see as a most precious heritage. She persuaded them they could sustain the vision by working together.

Not altogether convinced they would survive, they decided it hardly made a difference if they packed one more jug or one more woven cloth instead of a timbrel. If the timbrel signified hopefulness for Miriam, perhaps it could do the same for them. From her own experience, Miriam knew it was harder to imagine freedom than to sink into despair. She knew that sustaining hope was a most valuable gift she had, one she was able to share.

So the women packed timbrels. Each woman also packed an object that represented her own hopes for the future: garments for a baby yet to be conceived, a mold to cast jewelry for a bride, cloth for straining goat's milk to make enough cheese for a family.

Who could describe what they had all just witnessed as they crossed the sea into freedom? There was the bitter memory of years of slavery, the terrifying escape from Egypt, the armies that threatened their lives, and now, uncertainty. Was there really a promised land for them, a place they might reach before starving to death in the desert? Could their families recover enough from having lived in slavery, from memories of terror and violence, and the nightmares that continued to follow them, so vividly real? Could they ever be free enough to heal?

Miriam observed how fragile the women's joy was, how tentative. She too worried about the future, yet she refused to be overwhelmed. For herself, and for the women, Miriam struck a steady beat on her timbrel and sang a new song:

You have carried us over the water, enfolding us in strong and
  holy arms.
Held in this safe place, we celebrate:
this being free,
this never forgetting,
this prayer that we dance,
this life of holiness we will learn to embrace.

"Your souls dance with me, sisters! Come!" Miriam invited the girls
standing nearby to join in. While those women emerging from the sea
were still dazed by their survival, they allowed themselves to be
embraced by the widening circle of dancers. Verse by verse, the women
repeated Miriam's song until they knew the words and the melody by
heart. Oddly, it felt as if they had been singing it always, as if their lives
beforehand had been a rehearsal for this moment.

  In the background, the women heard the men singing a song of their
own, inspired by the song of Miriam. It was composed by Miriam's
brother Moses and led by her brother Aaron, by far the better singer:

I will sing to the Lord who has triumphed gloriously;
the horses and drivers have been hurled into the sea. . . .

As twilight fell, women improvised songs and dances of their own.
Miriam led them toward the men's circles. In the growing darkness, the
circles wove and intermingled. The movement slowed, and in the growing stillness of all their bodies, they could hear the same voice Miriam
had heard throughout the crossing, a voice that would echo among them
until the promise of a new, safe home was fulfilled:

You will be safe. You will be free. You will have a home. You will cele-
brate. You will never forget. You will be grateful always. You will live
each day in holiness. You will tell this story to your children, who will
tell it as their own.

Miriam spied a spring of fresh water not far off. She moved toward
the spring and knelt down to rinse her hands. She washed off the

darkness behind her and prepared for the light ahead. The others followed, washing their hands in the fresh water, cupping handfuls to drink. In this way, they prepared for the journey ahead.

Miriam Speaks to Us

Miriam tells us we have a choice. We can listen to those who confirm our anxieties that lead us to anticipate the worst, or we can listen to those who urge us to look toward a promising future. Miriam urges us: "Heed those voices that promote a promising vision and follow them!" She also tells us that we can be "Miriams" for others, offering the voice and example of inspiration, courage, and reassurance.

Miriam knows that what we imagine can come to pass—so why not imagine the future with optimism? She teaches us that it's not always possible for us to sustain optimism by ourselves. We need to seek out others who can inspire us, keep up our courage, and lead us to keep dreaming. Often, friends end up being "Miriams" for each other.

An interfaith hospital chaplain once told me a story about how she and a patient found a "Miriam" in one another.

The chaplain, on her daily rounds on the neurology unit, stopped to visit a woman in her early forties named Mara. The name Mara happens to be a version of Miriam, reflecting the Hebrew word *mara*, meaning "bitter." Given the news Mara had just received, she had reason to feel bitter about her future. Mara's doctors had told her that on account of her newly diagnosed disease, she would soon need to give up the kind of intensely physical work she had always done and loved to do—being a wilderness instructor. So there was the impending disability of the disease, which was enough to frighten Mara, and now the thought of being cut off from a whole part of who she was, her professional identity. "It's more than a job; it's my whole identity. It's what I love to do and how I'm known in the world," she told the chaplain.

The chaplain sat next to Mara's bed and listened to the story of how, when Mara first came into the hospital, a young resident working in the ER who looked no older than a high school boy had made the speedy diagnosis that may have in fact saved Mara's life. Mara felt she ought to be grateful for that. But the life that remained possible to her seemed so diminished. And if Mara was honest, being alive wasn't good enough if she couldn't believe she would be fully well again.

The chaplain could too easily imagine herself in Mara's shoes. Her mind raced: What if, for some reason, she had been the one who was told, "You can no longer visit patients and support their families as your ministry. Turn in your ID badge and white coat, relinquish your hospital parking pass, and look elsewhere for meaning in life." There were worse things that could happen to a person besides losing one's professional identity. Of this the chaplain was well aware: after the initial shock and denial passed, people adjusted. She had seen this often, people who refused to let real constraints—such as disability, paralysis, or chronic pain—close them down. But she just knew that if she herself were in the situation that Mara now faced, she could not sustain the loss. Without a family and hardly a social life outside the hospital, she felt that being a chaplain was all of who she was, all she ever wanted to be.

The chaplain strained to listen to Mara with openness, to trust she would find the right words to say. She coached herself as her supervising chaplain had mentored her years before when she was in pastoral training: "Your role is not to offer a solution, to make things better, or to apologize for God. Just be fully present."

When Mara said all she wished to share with the chaplain, they sat in silence for a good while. The chaplain was struck by the composure Mara now radiated. As a professional, the chaplain knew she could read this in two ways. Either Mara was in denial, or she was blessed with the strength of optimism to be able to trust she would move on. Maybe it was a little of both.

"Isn't this the part where you pray for me?" Mara asked, joking in tone, but it seemed to the chaplain that she was earnest in her request.

The chaplain asked if she might take Mara's hand, hoping the right prayer would come to her, as none of the conventional ones in her repertoire—the "God, please bring healing upon so-and-so who stands with me before You . . ." variety—felt right. This patient's predicament had thrown her, and she knew she needed to pray for herself as well.

Mara offered her hand. As the chaplain said the name Mara to herself, she recalled from her study of biblical Hebrew in seminary that the word *mara* also connoted "rising up," and she felt moved to share, as her prayer, the story of Miriam rising up in her now.

Mara said she knew the biblical story of Miriam—as well as Disney's *The Prince of Egypt,* in which Miriam appears as a cross between the Little Mermaid, Snow White, and Pocahontas. Mara knew some of the Miriam legends: The story of Miriam who had dreamt that her parents would have a baby who would perform wonders for the Children of Israel and lead them to freedom. The story of Miriam who had helped Pharaoh's daughter find a nursemaid (Moses's own mother!) to nurse the baby who had been set afloat in a basket in the Nile. And, of course, there was the "Miriam and the dancing girls" scene after the parting of the sea, which modern-day feminists of all stripes, beating drums or shaking tambourines at women's retreats, have embraced as a symbol of women's creative power, triumphantly unleashed at last.

The chaplain shared another Miriam story, one Mara didn't know. It was told that after the Israelites had been freed from Egypt and were crossing the desert, a well followed them, a magical well of Miriam. No matter where the Children of Israel went into the unknown, no matter how implausible it was that they would find fresh spring water, Miriam's presence assured them. As long as Miriam accompanied them, there would always be a wellspring of water upon which to draw. This miraculous well, given to the people in Miriam's honor, was said to have existed since the beginning of time. You'd have thought it was Miriam, gifted with dowsing skills, who had found the well, but that was not so. Miriam gave the people reason to believe they themselves would find the waters they needed to survive, and with such confidence, they were successful. In the legend, images of wells became waterways blossoming in the wilderness, and ladies floated up and down tributaries on lovely boats as they paid visits to one another, much like the watery extravaganzas in the court of Louis XIV. The core teaching remained: those who seek sustenance with optimism will have a chance of finding it.

Mara hadn't known the legend of the well, but she could see that it held truth for her.

"This story is my prayer for you," the chaplain said, knowing it was a prayer for herself as well. "May you be blessed, so that you, like Miriam, will seek and discover unexpected wells to draw water from—

sources of sustenance that come by surprise—no matter where your journeys take you."

"I know I will," Mara said, and as the chaplain readied to leave, she added, "And you would too, trust me. You would embrace the story of Miriam, just as you asked me to do. I can tell: you would allow yourself to be encouraged."

The chaplain lingered outside Mara's door. She had heard the voice of Miriam. They both had.

Embracing the Gift of Miriam

Who inspires you to stop fretting and start believing that everything will work out? Who allows you to believe that wherever your life's journey takes you, you will know how to find what you need and whom you need to sustain yourself? Who is the person who says, "I have confidence in you," in such a way that you trust yourself more and you feel possibility where otherwise you might have seen only closed doors? Who listens to your biggest dreams without laughing and resists calling them unrealistic or implausible, even when they might just be? Who pushes you to work harder and take larger chances even when bailing out or crawling back into bed seems more inviting? Who helps you to endure the inevitable setbacks and then stands with you until you can get back on course again? Who helps you to remember that you have the capacity to make enormous changes and still hold on to your core? Who helps you to laugh at yourself?

The sources of your inspiration, your Miriams, are never too far from you. You probably have multiple Miriams, spiritual midwives who encourage you in distinctive ways. I have one Miriam for spiritual dilemmas and another for ethical ones; I have one for literary blocks and another for administrative challenges; there is one for family dramas, one for healing, even a gardening Miriam who tells me, "Start as early as March with seedlings in your basement. And think big." I have a fashion Miriam who tells me that if I keep going back to Marshalls with an open mind, I will find a dress for my cousin's wedding. (I did, on the third try: I found two, as a matter of fact, and got them both.) Some of my Miriams inspire me by the lives they lead, others by the stories they tell, others by the advice they parcel out.

Your Miriam may not necessarily be the conventional wise woman from central casting. She might be a little girl in your community who looks up to you and thinks you can accomplish anything. She might be your next-door neighbor, who sees you in your driveway after a thunderstorm standing next to the tree that has fallen on your parked car, and who says, "You'll figure this out and you'll be grateful, because you know it could have been worse." Your Miriams are all the people who tumble into your life and provide you with vision and courage.

Note, too, who your "non-Miriams" are: They are the ones who ask you if it really is such a good idea to move, take a more demanding job, commit yourself to the one you love, or have another child. They're the ones who ask you, "Do you have any idea what you're doing?" as if having neither experience nor certainty were a recipe for failure. Theirs are the voices to silence.

To perform the ritual of Miriam, keep your Miriams close to you with a photograph or with their phone numbers or e-mail addresses in easy reach, and check in. Take care that you cherish your Miriams and support them, remembering that no one, despite appearances of hardiness and self-sufficiency—can continue to sustain others without being sustained herself. You would know this, because you are surely a Miriam too. For some, you may be a Miriam on constant call, and for others, a Miriam who appears on special occasions, like a fairy godmother. You must also protect your own capacity to be a Miriam: you can't be there inspiring everyone, full time. Every Miriam, once in a while, needs to lay down her timbrel and be replenished.

PART II

LIVING IN A WOMAN'S BODY

CHAPTER 4

THE DAUGHTERS OF TZLOFHAD
SPEAKING OUT IN A MAN'S WORLD

The Biblical Story

Now Tzlofhad, son of Hefer, had no sons, only daughters. . . . These daughters of Tzlofhad came forward. The names of the daughters were Mahlah, Noah, Hoglah, Milcah, and Tirzah. They stood before Moses, Eleazar the priest, the chieftains, and the entire community, at the entrance of the Tent of Meeting and they said, "Our father died in the wilderness . . . and he has left no sons. Why should our father's name be lost to his clan just because he had no son? Give us a holding among our father's brothers."

Moses brought their case before the Lord. And the Lord said to Moses: "The daughters of Tzlofhad speak justly. You should give them a hereditary claim among their father's brothers; transfer their father's inheritance to them. Further, speak to the Israelite people, saying, 'If a man dies without leaving a son, you shall transfer his inheritance to his daughter. . . . This shall be the law of procedure for the Israelites.'"

—Adapted from Numbers 26:33; 27:1–11

The Daughters of Tzlofhad's Own Story

The five sisters, daughters of Tzlofhad, had wanted to come early, to be the first in line at the Tent of Meeting to present their plea to inherit their father's estate. But each had unavoidable delays at home, and by the time all five met in front of their late father's tent and made it over to the Tent of Meeting, the line of petitioners was already snaking around. They hadn't even presented their case and already, as they moved to the end of the line, they were edgy with one another. It was going to be a long day; there was no way they could return home before nightfall. Fortunately, Mahlah had thought to bring cracked wheat bread she had baked the day before. She unwrapped it, breaking off a good-sized piece for each sister and for herself. Swallowing the hearty bread, they swallowed away the small angers caused by their late start and focused on their mission as they inched slowly forward.

Would they get past the functionary who heard the pleas? And if they did, who would take on their case? The elders of the community? Selected chieftains? Eleazar the priest? Perhaps Moses himself.

The sisters—united in this cause, but so different in talent and temperament—looked now to each other for support. They reached within themselves as well, for each had prepared to handle this day in her own way.

Hoglah had been sparklingly confident all along and remained so. She believed that what was right and fair would prevail; it was just a matter of bringing the injustice out in the open and speaking the truth. She had already prepared cakes, and she brought them with her so that they could celebrate as soon as they heard the good news. She had even written a poem of celebration, one that might be saved and passed on, and she had rehearsed it.

Tirzah knew how clearly Hoglah anticipated their success, and she hesitated to dampen Hoglah's enthusiasm, which was admittedly inspiring. But she thought Hoglah was naïve. Tirzah worried that Hoglah's confidence would lead her sisters to be more disappointed with an unfavorable decision than they would otherwise have been had they maintained the more sober, level-headed approach she favored. Their claim was just and the legal innovation they proposed was feasible and in keeping with existing practices, but she knew that didn't mean they would win. People resisted new ideas. A struggle such as theirs could take generations. Did she, personally, have the strength to keep fighting for years, if that's what it would take? She didn't know. Tirzah had long recognized the downside to her realism: it had kept her from being daring and caused her to settle for what was predictable, rather than what was possible.

Noah was the most legally astute and logically precise of the sisters. She was the one who pestered their father to teach her the legal codes of their people, which he'd have taught, without urging, to a son. She, in turn, had taught her sisters. Now Noah calmed herself by reviewing their strategy. When asked to present their complete argument, they would tell Moses that according to the laws and practices of levirate marriage, their mother, now a widow, was theoretically obliged to marry one of her deceased husband's brothers, thereby producing a male heir who would carry on her husband's name and inherit his property. But their mother could not legally bear her brother-in-law's child (even if she had wished to!) because she had already given birth to daughters. They, from the perspective of levirate marriage, were considered her husband's heirs. In conclusion, Noah repeated to herself, the existing laws of levirate marriage were flawed and contradictory. This should be made altogether clear to the tribunal. A daughter had to either count or not count as a legitimate heir. She couldn't be discounted as an heir when it came to inheritance and then be counted when it came to the levirate marriage laws. If the case could be heard according to its merits, it should be an open-and-shut matter.

Milcah was the most socially astute, reading people well. She believed that whatever merits their case had, their success depended on how it was presented and how it was heard. She knew how to deal well with functionaries and to speak confidently to those in power. Chameleon-like, she could flirt if she needed to, and didn't mind—she could play demure, pious, or be businesslike. Now she calculated how they would best appear before Moses.

Mahlah was the spiritual center for her sisters. After their father's death, she continued his practice of giving each a blessing on the Sabbath. As her loaves of bread nourished them, so did her blessings. She could find the precise words to draw each sister nearer to God, and in doing so, she brought them nearer to each other. She helped her sisters to remember that their putting all this effort into inheriting their father's land was more than a financial matter, even more than achieving justice. It was a matter of keeping their father and his ancestors so close that you could almost touch their presence. Their father's land was more than something to own or a place to live: it was history, it was memory, it was love, it was who they were and how they could stay whole.

Finally the functionary called them to approach the tent; he told them only one of them would be permitted to speak for the others. "If only that were possible," Milcah said, "we would be happy to comply." She took him aside and whispered that no one sister could tell the whole story—each knew only a part. The functionary accepted this and allowed all the sisters, one after the other, to present a portion of the case with her uniquely persuasive voice.

"Wait here," he told them, when they were through. They could hear their story being told and retold, like an echo. The functionary reappeared late in the afternoon: "Your case rests with Moses now."

The sisters waited until it was nearly nighttime. For Hoglah, the wait was a good sign and she broke out the cakes she had brought as a "pre-celebration celebration." For Tirzah, each moment that passed confirmed her sense that they should be bracing themselves for the worst, but she had, thus far, restrained herself from sharing the dimness of her hopes.

The functionary called each by name. "Follow me. I will bring you before Moses."

Moses sat alone and low to the ground. He looked weary. The functionary bid the sisters to repeat their story, to confirm what Moses had been told. Again, each spoke one part in her own voice.

"Then I have heard your story correctly. I cannot decide your case," he admitted. "No man can. Only the Holy One, who rules in justice and compassion, can do that."

As Moses entered the Tent of Meeting, the sisters prepared to return home, not knowing how long it would take for their case to reach the ear of God. But Moses emerged quickly from the tent and called them back. He seemed startled by the words that came out of his mouth, for they were not his own words, but the words of God:

"The Holy One has decided in favor of the daughters of Tzlofhad."

Hoglah reached for her poem.

The Daughters of Tzlofhad Speak to Us

I once heard of someone proposing to write a "Happy Bible," a rosy book of happy endings. In the version I imagined, God would tell Adam and Eve not to eat from a particular tree in the Garden of Eden and they would say, "No problem, we're allergic." The generation of Noah wouldn't really be evil, just a little rambunctious, and all the people and all the animals would get on the ark, two by two, and go for a lovely boat ride on a gentle lake. While aboard, they would all resolve to be better behaved. When the rainbow appeared in the sky, they would disembark in an orderly fashion, go home, get into pajamas, and fall fast asleep.

One story in the Bible needs no transformation for anyone's "Happy Bible," and that is the story of the daughters of Tzlofhad. We needn't squint, stand on our heads, or read between the lines to see it in a positive light. It is quite simply a happy story of women who succeed when they join together to protest an unjust social order and bring about dramatic change without much ado. The story would have been happy enough had God come onto the human landscape and proclaimed, "Listen up: There is a law on the books that's not fair to women. I'll fix that." What makes the story even happier is that it's about women who have the analytical eye and sense of entitlement to say, "Something is wrong here, and we are entitled and empowered to fix it." It's about women who have the voice to speak their minds, women who strategize to create a more just society, for themselves and for their descendents. And it is a story about women being heard, not only by the highest male authorities of their time, but also by God, who advocates on their behalf. Judith Baskin, in her book *Midrashic Women*, describes the daughters of Tzlofhad well. According to Baskin, they are "canny and competent women who trusted that divine mercy would transcend the mutable norms of a human society in which women were subordinate human beings."[1] They were "sisters, whose control of male knowledge allowed them to shape their own destinies. . . . [Their story] epitomize[s] an untainted instance of female empowerment . . ."[2]

The daughters of Tzlofhad are elegant role models for any group of women who join together in the name of justice and equality to take on rules that were established by men and that happen to favor men.[3] The daughters show us how women can work together to effectively be heard in settings that have traditionally privileged male styles of leadership and expression. The daughters show us that we can teach men to recognize and respect the different but highly effective ways that women working together can lead and make important changes. (They also remind us to pick our battles well.)

After their father died, no social mechanism existed for the five daughters of the Tzlofhad family to receive his inheritance or to perpetuate his name. Until the daughters challenged the status quo, all inheritance passed only from father to son. At this point in Israelite history, many of the laws had yet to be fleshed out by practice: this was the wilderness generation, a people who had been enslaved in Egypt and who, until now, had no property of their own to pass on. It was only when they were on the verge of coming into the land of Canaan that issues concerning the laws of inheritance were put into practice and were—at least by women—found to be wanting.

Erudite in matters of the law, the sisters refused to accept a practice that was inherently unfair. A law that made women vulnerable was a law that ought to be changed. They had faith in their community's justice system and their right to challenge and change it.

Moses, seeing that this issue was larger than anything he and his colleagues could handle, brought the case to the highest authority, God. God heard the women's argument and acknowledged that the law needed to be amended so that women without brothers could indeed count as legitimate heirs. Not surprisingly, men challenged God's radically new law that made women completely equal as inheritors. To quiet the men's complaints, the law was modified: daughters could inherit, but they were obliged to marry men within their tribe (their cousins, that is) lest their marrying out reduce the tribal holdings in the next generation. The daughters of Tzlofhad accepted this constraint—at least they could freely choose the cousins they wished to marry—acknowledging that in a given generation, one can push the social order to stretch only so far.

The daughters offer seven strategies for women who organize together to speak out against injustices and make change. We need to remember their strategies and continue to use them, for despite the enormous changes in status women have achieved in the past decades, it remains a man's world. Men still tend to set policies, and men in power are still more apt to heed male voices. These strategies have worked for women who have joined together for such causes as women's voting rights, coeducation, women's health care, equity in employment policies, and maternity and family-care policies. Not surprisingly, we can rarely name individual women who achieved these major changes, for they were the result of women—often nameless—working together. They put the cause over personal gain.

The first strategy: present a unified public voice expressing solidarity and resolve. We don't hear the daughters of Tzlofhad quibbling in public about who deserves a bigger portion of her father's inheritance. Did these squabbles take place behind the scenes? Probably. One daughter loved her father more, one took care of him more, one was loved better than the others, one had a sick husband . . . But the daughters aired their personal differences in private. And then they shelved their disagreements, formulating a strategy and a goal they could all endorse.

The second strategy: divide the work equally but according to the particular gifts and passions of each person. Each of the daughters presented a different aspect of their case that she was best suited to articulate; each spoke confidently out of the reality of her own lived experience.

The third strategy: aim for good timing. The daughters acted expeditiously, forcefully, and at the opportune moment. They were alert to winds of change. As soon as they heard that the land was to be divided among the tribes, according to male members alone, the sisters knew they had a brief window of opportunity to address female inheritance. They seized the moment. Had they waited, the land would have been divided and they would have had no recourse. In one ancient legend, we learn that the daughters were alert to the benefits of good timing by bringing their argument before Moses and the tribunal precisely at the time that the issue of inheritance was already being discussed. When an issue is on people's minds and is the subject of fresh public debate, there is greater openness to hearing related, urgent concerns. When the topic loses its novelty, when people have decided it has ceased to matter, it becomes harder to get it back on the agenda. (Advertisers of items that help people control their anxieties know this well. When kidnappings are in the news, people selling security systems and guard dogs have a rapt audience. When the news shifts to epidemics, sellers of surgical masks and home entertainment claim our attention.)

The fourth strategy: be fully aware of existing policies and the mechanisms by which change happens. Being on the side of the right and good is insufficient assurance you will succeed in making social change. Most institutions fear and resist change, if only because it's unfamiliar. The daughters, exceptionally wise, knew their Scripture. More than that, they knew how to interpret it so that it could be realistically applied to daily life. They knew how to speak within the system to support their claim for female inheritance. There was no pulling wool over their eyes. This has been the case of the Women of the Wall, a group I have belonged to, fighting in the Israeli Supreme Court against the State of Israel for fourteen years now for the right to pray as men do at the Western Wall, a remnant of the ancient Temple in Jerusalem, which many consider Judaism's holiest site. It remains illegal for women to pray aloud, wear prayer shawls, and read from a Torah scroll. The Women of the Wall have not relied on male scholars of Scripture or male agents of change in order to formulate their case. It is their own learning and legal know-how that they rely on. Despite multiple setbacks, the case continues to be fought.

The fifth strategy: choose lines of argument calculated to appeal to those in power. Know your audience. The daughters didn't claim the right to inheritance in the name of justice. Had they done so, they would have been written off. Instead they said, "Why should the name of our father be done away from his family because he has no sons?" They gave those sitting in judgment a scenario they could relate to. They appealed to any man with only daughters, concerned to have his name perpetuated. They put their argument in language that the men found familiar. I know of a group of women who did this well when they organized to find a way to expel the young assistant principal of a church school—quite the misogynist—who was alienating more and more girls and their mothers each day. The women wanted him out. They went before the priest who was the headmaster to present their complaint. He attempted to silence them, saying, "We should see this young man as a gift from God, sent to us to teach us a lesson." The women had a great response. They said they were prepared to act self-lessly in "regifting" this young man to another school better able to appreciate him.

The sixth strategy: value the autonomy that having property bestows upon a woman. The women did not ask for honor or titles. They wanted financial stability, knowing that with such a base, they could be inde-pendent adults, freer of control than they would otherwise have been.

The final, seventh strategy: expect that you deserve the support and even sacrifices of your family when your belief in a cause is great. To achieve their rights (and the rights of all their children), the daughters had to spend time away from home in order to plan and present their case at the Tent of Meeting. Justifying time spent away from home and family remains hard for many women. Gloria Steinem offers a com-pelling explanation: "Unlike men, who are actually praised for leaving their families to fight for what they believe in—no matter how distant or arcane their cause—women are called selfish if we fail to sacrifice *everything* for our families or if we even speak up for ourselves."[4] This doesn't mean that our families won't grumble about the loss of our attention, but it does mean that we can learn not to let their grumbling restrict our activism.

Embracing the Gift of the Daughters of Tzlofhad

Women gathering together to effect change in the world can perform the ritual of the daughters of Tzlofhad the first time their group meets, and can repeat it on subsequent gatherings. With each repetition, it will become even dearer, as it starts to reflect the identity and personality of the group.

This simple ritual affirms your commitments to each other and to your cause. It can help you to acknowledge that in the process of your working together, there will inevitably be arguments, and it allows you to affirm that you can surmount the disagreements and the acrimony. It helps acknowledge that while each woman has a distinctive voice and a distinctive vision of her desired outcomes, not every voice and every perspective can ultimately be represented. The ritual helps you keep together and keep your eyes on your goal.

Mark your coming together by breaking bread. If someone can bake a loaf for the group each time, all the better, as you will feel particularly nurtured by the love and effort of each baker.

Before breaking off a piece for each woman present and for herself, the baker offers a blessing:

> *Before we begin our work together, we break bread, symbol of life, of work, and of a long process that begins with a small seed and is transformed by divine grace and our own hard labor.*
>
> *Blessed is the source of this bread and all that we need to sustain us in our journey together. As we are sustained by bread, may we also be sustained by our collective wisdom, our friendship, our intimacy, our courage, and our vision. May our journey together, however it unfolds, be a source of blessing.*

At your first meeting, you might also open up a bottle of wine and make a toast, celebrating this group of women who have come together to achieve a common vision.

CHAPTER 5

THE WOMAN OF VALOR
REPAIRING THE WORLD
IN YOUR OWN WAY

The Biblical Story

Who might find a valorous woman, whose worth far exceeds pearls?
Her husband trusts her deeply and he lacks for no riches.
Each day she merits her family only good and never evil.
She seeks wool and flax and gladly works with her hands.
She would trade like a sea merchant in order to obtain goods for
*   her family.*
She awakens late in the night to provide food for her family and
*   wages for her staff.*
She surveys land and acquires it, and grows a vineyard from her
*   labor.*
She keeps herself strong, and her arms are powerful.
She ensures her business dealings are successful and keeps her light
*   on at night.*
Her hands work the spinner and keep a firm grip on the spindle.
Her arms are open to the poor and she is generous to the destitute.
She does not fear for her family in the cold, for they are clothed in
*   wool.*
She makes her own carpets and wears clothing of white and purple.
Her husband is known in the city, where he meets with the elders.
She makes cloths for the markets and sells belts to the merchants.
She exudes strength and dignity and radiates joyous optimism.

Her mouth drips of wisdom and her words are kindness.
She maintains the decorum of her house and knows not of sloth.
Her children strive to please her and her husband to praise her.
Many are the women who have demonstrated valor, but you surpass them all.
Charm can be false, and beauty a ruse, but a God-fearing woman is truly praiseworthy.
Give due credit to her works and celebrate her through her accomplishments.

—Proverbs 31:10–31[1]

The Woman of Valor's Own Story

She is the daughter of a woman so remarkable that people call her "the woman of valor's daughter." Every day she watches her mother go out into the world, and it makes her head ache. People say, "Oh, you must be so proud of your mother," and of course she is proud, because how can she not be? There is nothing her mother cannot do. And how can she not feel grateful, too, to a person who is so accomplished, so generous, so attentive to what each member of the family is feeling and needing—someone altogether not filled with herself?

But then when people say, "I'm sure you want to be just like your mother," she is quite sure she does not. Continual excellence is just too much pressure, and so is unending altruism and self-abnegation. She would rather try her best most of the time, but not always (for she might feel tired or not be in the mood); she is happy to lend a hand, but on her own terms. She plans to be the kind of person who is so shocked when things go well that she celebrates, a person who occasionally makes a total mess of things and then forgives herself handsomely.

She prefers not to be judged poorly or even judged well, as her mother is judged continually. She prefers not to be measured or scrutinized at all. She wants to live her life and be surprised by what happens next. She wants to be valued for herself and not for her accomplishments. Couldn't that be enough?

Her mother returns home, exhausted by her day. The daughter can see how her mother's nerves are frayed. Her mother has never before let her see just how drained she is at the end of the day; she has always covered it over. For the daughter, seeing this side of her mother is a gift, and she thanks her mother for showing her this view of valor.

The Woman of Valor Speaks to Us

The woman of valor, whom we meet in the Book of Proverbs, is a cornucopia of admirable traits, a superwoman who inspires those yearning to make a difference in the world.

Consider her. Inviting trust, she can always be counted on. Consistently wise, she is always heeded. She loves working, rolling up her sleeves and getting involved. She surveys land, plants and runs a vineyard, spins wool, weaves cloth, and makes belts and clothing. A fine businesswoman, she gets her goods to the market and makes a profit, all while treating her workers fairly and with respect. And however busy, she meets all the needs of her family. She is inherently strong—both in physical power and strength of will. She is a real role model.

But is she the only role model?

The woman of valor cautions us that there are alternative models for women's lives, other inspirational life stories of women who have made a difference. "The stories of role models that you grew up with," she tells us, "may be outdated. Or they may not be right for you. Find a script that works for who you are." Paraphrasing the feminist writer Monique Wittig, she might say, "If the script you need is lacking, invent it."

For centuries, many a husband has chanted the proverb about the woman of valor to his wife to demonstrate his appreciation. He says, "I've noticed all that you've done for us."

Some women prefer not to have this proverb recited in their honor, and it's easy to see why. There is the housewifely image: the woman who is selfless, who works her fingers to the bone, and who privileges others' needs over her own. If these traits were so admirable, wouldn't we hold them up for men as well? Why do we readily reward a woman's caregiving roles and her selflessness and, typically, ignore or suspect her other traits—say, independence, tenacity, fearlessness, and courage? These traits seem to be praised only when a woman uses them for the benefit of others—when she is courageous and fearless in protecting her family, but not when she is taking care of herself.

For all the difference the woman of valor makes, it's interesting that no one knows her name. Only her husband is known outside their domestic world; it is he who has power and influence. I am reminded of an expression often heard when an accomplished woman accompanies her husband in public and is introduced as "a person in her own right." It's meant well—the speaker intends to say, "In case you didn't know, so-and-so's wife is a person of substance as well"—but just the same, it maintains the outdated assumption that until you hear otherwise, wives are accessories.

For a long time, I resisted seeing the woman of valor as a role model, for many of the reasons just stated. Encountering her now, she bids me to reconsider. She has achieved what so many of my women friends want: a great family and compelling work. She stays home and bakes cookies *and* is out there in the world, interacting with merchants, transforming the landscape, bringing the moral weight that characterizes her private life into her dealings in the world. She has emotional fulfillment, ample creative outlets, and financial stability. People listen to her and allow her to influence them.

To accept the woman of valor as a valid role model, I must hear her admitting that her successes are possible only because she builds on her many advantages. There is the matter of her social position. She is someone's wife, and her husband is well respected. She is someone's mother, and her children appear to be sources of joy. She has a home, enough food, possessions, fine clothes, paid assistants, and access to people of influence. If she lacks something, she has the resources and know-how with which to create it. She has good health and ample energy. Anyone who is single, gay, childless, unemployed, disabled, poor, or socially marginalized in any respect will feel herself not represented.

To see the woman of valor as a role model, I need to hear in her voice the downside of her daunting goodness and selflessness: She does not make meeting her own needs a priority. She works constantly and doesn't know how to stop. She feels too guilty to rest, and as enticing as recreation might be, she can't stop judging it as a waste of time. She has come to measure herself, as others do, by her accomplishments.

If the woman of valor were to become unable to work in her customary way, would she have another sense of identity to fall back on? Predictable and even-tempered, would she still be loved if she exploded, flew off the handle, panicked, or became depressed? What if she lived in a flawed system she believed needed changing? What if she decided the culture she lived in was unjust, unfair, deplorable? Could she develop a whole new set of traits? Could she be a judge, a warrior, a critic, a provocateur, a narrator, a holy woman?

Let us imagine a different kind of woman of valor, one who expresses the variety of ways a woman can be active in the world and still be respected. One who challenges, and does not affirm, the social order and the status quo; one who, when recognizing that the needs of women are still unmet and the poor are still poor, challenges the very system that creates and sustains neediness.

In 1994, author Esther Broner adapted "The Woman of Valor" to describe an alternative vision of an ideal woman:

Who can find a wise woman?
For her price is far above rubies.
Those in her house safely trust her
For she heeds the words of her children,
She works alongside her husband,
But outside the walls of her house,
Outside the gates of her garden,
She hears the cries in the city,
The cries of women in distress.
She is their rescuer.

She rises at dawn to organize.
She rises before light to make orderly the day.
She stretches out her hand to unchain
The chained woman,

The woman without recourse,
The women not paid their worth on this earth.

She taketh on the men at the gate,
The men of the law-making bodies,
The men of the Bet Din,
The Judges on high.
She looks them in the eye
and says:

This is unacceptable.
This is unjust.
This is cruel.
. . .
In her house she is praised.
In the state she is extolled.
Many women have done wisely
But she excels them all.[2]

Broner's tribute to the woman of valor reminds me of a time, back in the early nineties, when I was at a weeklong conference of feminist scholars and clergy held at a retreat center in California. We took what was intended to be a brief late-night break from our study. We wandered outside and sat on some bleachers and sang haunting melodies in the glimmer of the light of a full moon. A woman named Pam taught us a new song, and once we got started singing it, we couldn't stop. We sang till our voices were hoarse and we needed to huddle together to keep warm. The song was based on a single verse in the "Woman of Valor" proverb. As the story goes, the melody was created as a wedding present by a Hasidic father too poor to give his daughter anything else. Most of the song was wordless melody. Pam translated the few words from the Hebrew: "She is clothed with strength and splendor; she looks to the future cheerfully."

Pam asked us to try to move beyond the ways this proverb had once annoyed many of us. "Focus on the first words, 'clothed with strength,'" she told us, "and envision the many ways that women help themselves feel more powerful."

We had so many examples: We empower ourselves by wearing clothes and carrying briefcases that project an image of authority and accomplishment. We gain power from nurturing friendships, earning advanced degrees, learning self-defense, becoming physically strong or financially secure, and creating job environments that are comfortable for women. We gain power keeping our own names, or taking them back.

After we had sung some more, Pam suggested to us that the woman of valor, in "looking to the future cheerfully," also has the last laugh. What does it mean to be a woman who has the last laugh? It means you keep your energies focused, despite doubts and temporary setbacks, because you believe that in the end, good will prevail. It means you eventually get to feel smug when you've achieved your goals, however much others doubted you or you doubted yourself.

The woman of valor alerts us: many different kinds of personalities can be effective world repairers. This is a lesson learned from Exodus 30:34, in which God commands Moses that each day, incense must be burned in the holy temple for worship. That incense should contain equal portions of these specific spices: stacte, onycha, frankincense, and galbanum. Galbanum? Galbanum smells awful! Nonetheless, when it is combined with the other spices, it contributes to a fragrance that is holy and pure. This biblical verse has been used to teach that even people with those character traits we think of as flawed, quirky, or even obnoxious (like the galbanum) can be, especially in the context of a team effort, tremendous assets to the group. You may be glad you have a teammate with an obsessive-compulsive personality who sees to it that details are checked and rechecked. You want a worrier who anticipates problems and prepares for how they can be solved. You want a quiet listener who attends to what goes unsaid and reads nonverbal cues. You want the loud extravert who galvanizes social energy, and you want the person who never forgets to remember the pitfalls of the past. Were we all just pleasant, we'd be in big trouble.

The woman of valor implores us to praise admirable women of all sorts for whatever gifts they bring to the mix. Praise those who have no children of their own but still are nurturers. Praise women who resist long-term commitments but are still friends you can count on. Praise women whom you trust will be there for you occasionally, even if they are unpredictable. Praise women, footloose citizens of the world, who resist being pinned down. Praise women who are willing to pay the price for their unconventionality. Praise women who are loud trouble-makers. And praise women who very discreetly make all the difference.

Embracing the Gift of the Woman of Valor

The woman of valor's ritual might surprise you. It's about praise, but not the praise you receive from others for your obvious gifts. It's about praising yourself for your imperfections and seeing them in a new light—as virtues that can help you make a difference in the world. The ritual presents an opportunity for generous self-reflection and recalls the square-dance caller who announces it's time to bow, as you first "Honor your partner!" and then turn to the person on your other side and "Honor your corner!" Life presents us ample opportunities for self-critique and self-improvement. This time, you tip your hat to yourself, honoring just the way you are, with all your imperfections, real or imagined.

To perform the woman of valor's ritual, give yourself time to reflect on a trait or tendency you have that annoys you or threatens to trip you up. Perhaps it's a quality that gets in your way (such as needing to be hyperorganized) or makes you ashamed (such as stuttering); maybe it's a stereotypical assumption you can't shake, such as, "Things always go wrong for me." At some point in the future, you might choose to address your imperfections and eliminate them from your repertoire. But not now. Now you get to discover a way to honor all of who you are. Regard troublesome traits with new respect. See how they, like the galbanum included within the sacred incense, might be considered assets, particularly in the context of a group project (which might be a project outside the home or the enormous project of raising and sus-taining a family).

Imagine, for example, that your mettlesome trait is the feeling that however hard you try, you're never going to do the job well enough to satisfy everyone. What if you were to honor, and not bemoan, that trait? You might see that feelings of inadequacy and overwhelming self-critique can have positive implications. Fearing failure, you may reach out for help and pull others in to cooperate on your projects. It may mean that people count on you to leave no stone unturned, so aware are you of potential glitches. It may mean that in striving for remarkably high goals for yourself, you set the bar for others who are inspired by your vision and your tireless quest for excellence. It may mean that you are delightfully modest, considering you rarely give yourself credit for the contributions you make.

To recall the reflective work you have done, you might take a flat stone and, using a permanent marker, write on one side the mettlesome trait, and on the other, a word reminding you of how that trait can be a blessing. Keep it in your pocket and it will keep you strong.

CHAPTER 6

ESTHER
SETTING ONE'S OWN STANDARDS OF BEAUTY

The Biblical Story

The servants of King Ahasuerus advised him to find a new queen. "Appoint officers to bring all the beautiful virgins of Shushan to your palace. Provide them with cosmetics. Let the young woman who pleases you most become your new queen, replacing Vashti."

At this time, a Jew by the name of Mordechai, who lived in the walled city of Shushan, had become the foster father of his niece Hadassah, known as Esther, who had lost both her father and her mother. This young woman was altogether beautiful. When the king's order was proclaimed, many young women were brought to the king's palace. Esther, too, was taken into the women's chamber of the king's palace, and like the others, she was supervised by Hegai, guardian of the women. She had made a fine impression on him, and because he had taken to her, he hurried to provide her with all the cosmetics and things she might need, as well as with seven maids. He treated her and her maids kindly, looking out for them. Esther revealed her Jewish identity to no one, following her uncle's advice.

Before going before the king, each young woman was to engage in a twelve-month period of beautification (six months of oil of myrrh, six months with perfume and cosmetics). Whatever she asked for would be given. When it was Esther's turn to go before the king, she asked for nothing, only what Hegai had advised. Nonetheless, all who saw her admired her.

Esther was taken to King Ahasuerus in his royal palace. He loved Esther more than all the other women, and she attracted him more than any other. He placed a royal crown on her head and made her his queen, and he made a great banquet, the banquet of Esther.

—Adapted from Book of Esther 2

Esther's Own Story

When Esther was a child, people who had traveled from outside the town of Shushan would stop her Uncle Mordechai in the marketplace, commenting, "She is so beautiful!" as if she were an arresting cape he wore or an enchanting pet, ignoring that she had ears of her own, and feelings too. Esther, not content to be admired and move on, engaged her admirers in conversation, asking questions that started blandly enough: "Who are you and where do you come from?" She then drew them out: "What brought you here? Whom do you love that you've left behind? What do you dream of?" Disarmed, flattered to be taken so seriously, her admirers would reveal deep stories that displayed, to their surprise, the most precious parts of themselves. Only then did Esther release them. Needless to say, having been so noticed by Esther, they found her even more richly alluring.

In the summer of Esther's eighteenth year, Mordechai witnessed it once again. Evening was coming, and he hurried to the marketplace to accompany Esther back home after she had spent the day selling honey. As Mordechai helped Esther gather her things, an old woman who had come from out of town to sell wool, homeward bound herself, tapped Mordechai's shoulder.

"She is so beautiful—she must permit me to touch her cheek."

Even in the startling azure and crimson twilight of this night, Esther's appearance astonished. You wanted to touch her to confirm what you saw with your own eyes, to dispel its being illusory. Her beauty pulled you close, even in its starkness. Black shining hair, skin the color of light myrtle leaves, white cheeks like jasmine blossoms, almond eyes holding the shine of the stars. There was the sadness she carried of her parents' deaths that muted her beauty, and there was her own reticence, as well, the charm of her modest self-possession. And there was that gift of hers, the ability to draw others out and to discover their beauty, however concealed.

However frequently Esther drew attention, Mordechai assumed that even if Esther gazed at a hundred mirrors, she would not grasp how beautiful others found her. She hardly fussed over herself as women were said to, though he did remember when Esther and her girlfriends used to try, without much art, to rim their eyes with kohl; they ended up looking more sleepy than lovely. He imagined Esther might even think of herself as plain. Her regimen, to the best of his knowledge (and did he really know?), seemed spare. She splashed water on her face and kept herself shaded from the midday sun.

"Allow us to pass, please, woman!" Mordechai announced. Esther laughed quietly and parted her scarf with the fingers of her left hand as if she were opening a curtain to daylight, accepting the wool seller's soft, puffy fingers grazing against her face. Esther asked the old woman to put down her bundle and sit a moment along the side of the road. "Tell me who you are and to whom you belong," she said, and the woman's face opened. Mordechai, having practiced patience for such inevitable encounters, leaned against a tree and recalled the text of a scroll he was considering. It would be a while before they resumed their walk home.

The old woman told Esther her life story and tacked on a bit of gossip: the king was seeking a new queen, a beauty. "Go," she added. "You can draw him out."

Mordechai was taken aback when Esther announced later that night that she would leave for the king's palace at the sound of the first birdsong and compete among the beautiful young women of Shushan for the king's favor.

"Why would you do that?" Mordechai asked, his first "why" ever, because Esther, so transparent, hardly ever needed to explain.

"Beauty opens doors," she said, revealing she had indeed been aware of her beauty all along and possessed, moreover, a worldliness Mordechai had never noticed. This beauty of hers, she explained, had never been relevant before—just something pleasant to have and enjoy, a grace like a sweet voice or strong legs that were slow to tire. Esther said her beauty would give her leverage, allowing her to establish herself in the palace so that she would have the opportunity to . . . Esther couldn't pin down what the opportunity was that she envisioned. She felt as if her beauty qualified her for some mission demanding her presence and her gifts. Precisely what it was, she didn't know. She would listen for clues.

Before dawn, Esther packed a small bundle of her possessions, including the pot of kohl that had been her mother's and several jars of her honey. From the garden, she cut three twigs of the myrtle, her namesake. She told Mordechai, "I will root the twigs in water. They will remind me of where I came from and to whom I belong."

Escorting her to the palace, Mordechai wondered: How could I have been so convinced Esther was oblivious to her beauty and any leverage it might give her? Was it because she was kindhearted, worrying that a neighbor's child never had a change of clothes and making a robe for the child out of a shawl that had belonged to her own mother? Because she was wise, always anticipating which friend could be trusted? Because she was practical, always sensing which yeast was too old to rise?

Inside the walls of the palace, Esther quickly learned that the king's courtiers expected the young women who presented themselves to submit to a rigid schedule of beauty treatments. For the face, exfoliation with ground cinnamon bark and walnut shells, cleansing lotions and oil of myrrh, layers of colored powder. For the body, hot and icy baths, followed by soaks in warm water strewn with rose petals, almond and chamomile lotions, massages, pumice for knees and elbows. For the hair, a thousand brushstrokes, shampoos with duck eggs and milk, rinses with lavender, pomades of beeswax and honey, and elaborate plaiting. To all this, most women acquiesced, often with pleasure. Some introduced their own innovations from home: a perfume made from the roses and mallow from a mother's garden, eye compresses made from the cucumbers of a witch, applications of lime to soften the skin, depilatories of the oil of unripe olives. Some women made large batches of their home treatments and shared them; others guarded their ingredients and the practices of application. Esther found the process tedious, but she enjoyed the company of the other women and easily elicited stories from them all.

After a year of beautification, to Esther's mind, no one really looked much better. If anything, they all looked more alike, as if all the treatments homogenized them, obliterating the little flaws that had once given them distinction. The routine had become tiresome, and it registered on many a face as jadedness. Many were simply homesick.

Esther stared into her hand mirror, a piece of equipment each had been issued, and sat on the edge of the piles of silken spreads and woolen blankets in her corner of the women's chamber. How she too yearned for home. Who was she anymore, and to whom did she belong? Her story, her dreams—did the beauty of her face reveal any of that? What had propelled her to imagine that her particular beauty could touch a king's heart when all the others were, each in her own way, equally exquisite?

Some women prayed, and Esther did too. Esther prayed to God for success, which was, after all, the whole point, but she also prayed to be kept from being swallowed up by her loneliness, and she prayed that she would remember to wake up each day, able to hold on to her sense of mission. She prayed God would show her how to use the gift of her beauty to pull the king toward her and not to frighten him and push him away, because beauty could do that, too.

Soon she would be called to the king to have her brief encounter with him. Esther fasted. She lit several small oil lamps. She looked into the lights as if they were stars, asking for her mother's blessing.

As the day approached, the attendants pleaded more intensely with Esther: "The others have asked for special perfumes, balms, ointments. We have satisfied them, but you ask for nothing. Tell us what we may bring you."

But she needed nothing, she maintained, and not out of vanity. She didn't have to be the most beautiful; she couldn't be. After all, given the differences in taste, there were no objective standards for beauty. She needed for the king to experience her as being more beautiful than the others. That would happen only if she could know something about the king that would make him beautiful in *her* eyes.

In a scroll she kept to record her experiences in the king's palace, she wrote this down for herself to remember: "I look into your eyes. You think I am beautiful, but it is because you are beautiful to me. In this circle, we become precious to each other."

The attendants pestered her still, explaining that even a radiant beauty that got noticed in the marketplace needed some artifice for presentation in the gold-walled, sunlit chambers of the king. Relenting, Esther prepared a list of her needs: a bolt of blue silk, out of which she would stitch a sheath that would reflect like blue water; more honey from her bees, which she would rub into her hands and face to have the smell of home in her soul; and stories—she needed stories about the king.

"Tell me the story of the king's kindnesses, his simplicity, his generosity. What frightens him, what keeps him awake?" She knew what was common knowledge: that the king was sometimes foolish and cruel. But there had to be moments of goodness that could be recalled. Perhaps he had pardoned a street child who stole rolls, perhaps he had comforted the widow of one of his ministers with the gift of a caged songbird?

One attendant, known to augur the future, took Esther aside. "There is no story of the past that will excite your soul in the way you wish. But hear this story that will transpire: One day, the king's life will be threatened, and he will be saved by the intervention of your Uncle Mordechai. The king will show his gratitude by honoring Mordechai with a parade. The king will open a doorway for you, which you must pass through, and if you are bold enough, and if your God protects you, he will allow you to save many lives."

Esther listened, nodding along. Yes, Esther knew, this was the story she could hold in her heart.

On the morning she was to be brought into the king's presence, she was awakened while it was still dark. Attendants slapped her cheeks to heighten her color. Esther did not anticipate the terror she now felt, the shallow reach of her breath. She was glad she had cut sprigs of myrtle to tuck in her sleeve and honey to rub into her hands. Bringing her hands to her face, she smelled the familiarity of home and she could feel her heart pounding less heavily.

Esther asked to be permitted to stand outdoors in the fresh air for a few moments, away from the perfumes of the harem and court so she could feel the breeze, even though it would be disheveling. She could see the tips of the trees outside the palace walls fluttering from the weight of resting sparrows. While she yearned to be chosen, to follow this path along which she seemed to be led, she could also see there was a world of other paths should this one not work out. This openness, this belief in multiple possibilities unfolding, allowed her to breathe again. Returning, she felt steadied, as if held up and escorted by angels. Connected to home, confident about the future, had she ever been more beautiful?

She had been instructed to stand directly before the king, and she did this, even though he was looking away from her toward his windows. She was not permitted to speak until he did. Before he would turn toward her, before he would allow her to catch his eyes, she repeated to herself: "This is a man who will honor the dignity of my uncle. This is a man who will give me the opportunity to take extraordinary risk."

When the King first regarded Esther, he saw a woman who was as beautiful as all the others. Then he looked into her eyes. While he was not sensitive enough to see the beauty of Esther's character or the subtleness of her presence, he found her altogether arresting. She was the most beautiful of all because, through her eyes, he could see the best image of himself. This was the beauty that won his heart.

Esther Speaks to Us

When we first meet Esther, she is a pretty orphan girl who wins a beauty contest and becomes the new queen of King Ahasuerus. Her beauty ceases to matter as we watch her use her intelligence and influence with the king to undo the plans of a government official plotting to annihilate her people. But Esther's beauty shouldn't be dismissed as only being instrumental.

Beauty is an asset to use well, a gift like intelligence, faith, physical strength, creative talents, wealth, or having the right connections. Beauty opens doors, and such access can be used for the good. We all know that the initial allure of beauty fades unless it is augmented by substance. Esther reminds us that the substance behind her beauty was her capacity to be intrigued by others, to pull out the best in them, and to reflect it back for them to see. For others, the substance might be an infectious confidence about the future. It could be laughter. It could be endless compassion.

Esther was beautiful by the conventions of her culture. She knew that being thought beautiful was a blessing. It made her feel good about herself, and it drew people to her, making her feel success and accomplishment for having done nothing at all. She was also aware that people found her beautiful for reasons that had little to do with her appearance. She could access the beauty of the other and radiate it back. It was this conviction—that beauty was a two-way matter—that gave Esther the courage to find her way into the palace of Shushan and the heart of the king.

We can draw on Esther's gift of being able to reflect back the beauty of others when we prepare ourselves to encounter people we want to connect to. I remember getting ready to go to the theater one night to see a play and then meet with the theater director who had read a script of mine and was considering me for a grant to develop material for his company. I had flown into New York for this meeting and was staying at my parents' house that weekend. I went madly through the upstairs cedar closet where my sister and I had left odds and ends of clothing even after we had both married and left home. I was hoping I would find something that would make me look more writerly, more artsy and alluring—essentially more *anything* than I actually was, which was five months pregnant and feeling frumpy and drained (the radiant part had yet to happen). The pickings in the closet were slim: my peasant blouses and granny dresses from the sixties; my sister's assortment of prom gowns and puffy sherbet-colored bridesmaid's dresses from the seventies. All smelled so strongly of cedar that even if I found something that looked right, I'd smell as if I had come out of a gerbil's cage. My father, hearing me stomping around, came upstairs and offered his advice.

"You will look beautiful no matter what you wear." (This I doubted, but what was he going to say?) Sounding very much the salesman he was, he said I needed to have confidence and project confidence, because the theater director was as afraid of me as I was of him. All I had to do was help him feel good about himself. Then he'd feel good about me, and everything would turn out just fine.

Only a father who loved his daughter too well and had an unrealistic sense of her gifts would say that. I was meeting a well-known director. He hardly needed a young, unknown writer to bolster his self-esteem.

My father then offered to take me to Loehman's and help me pick out something flattering. I accepted. We went and found nothing. Back home, now foraging in my mother's closet, I found a black velvet dress she had worn to her brother's wedding. She tied an orange chiffon scarf around my neck, saying that now I looked artsy. (I must have looked like a pregnant black cat, dolled up for Halloween.)

In the taxi to the theater, I decided I might as well try out my father's advice, still believing that if it worked at all, it only worked in business and not in the arts. As I watched the performance, I practiced formulating kind things I could say to the director afterward. That was easy enough, as the play was witty and engaging. After the show, I went down the aisle (I felt like I waddled, but this was probably not the case), and when the circle of people congratulating the director thinned, I angled myself in and spilled out all the praise I had rehearsed.

"Do you really mean that?" he asked me, taking me aside, asking for elaboration. "It means so much, coming from you."

I felt altogether lovely at that moment, and smart too. (Apparently the director knew how to use the gift of Esther as well.) I got the grant and it made a huge difference in increasing my self-confidence. I was most grateful to my father for his incredible insight.

Embracing the Gift of Esther

Each morning you probably pace through your own beauty routine as you get ready to face the day. You might see putting on makeup as a ritual that helps you to gird your loins for a challenging day, making you feel more confident and attractive. On the other hand, you may question why you even go along with the curious social convention that urges women to paint their lips red, heighten the rosiness of their cheeks, exaggerate the contours of the eye, and camouflage flaws with foundation and powder. You may ask, if men can go out as God made them (until recently, that is, now that cosmetics for men are being sold), why not women?

Consider trying out Esther's beauty ritual. It's simple enough. Begin by turning away from the mirror after you have completed getting ready for the day in whatever way makes you feel good about yourself. Then, think about the people whom you plan to encounter in the course of the day. Imagine them and recall what it is about them that you admire. Think of specific details: the inner peace and grace of your yoga instructor; the ability of a coworker to make puns; your brother-in-law's sense of responsibility. Then repeat Esther's chant: "I look into your eyes. You think I am beautiful, but it is because you are beautiful to me. In this circle, we become precious to each other." When you see these people whose special gifts you've imagined, do not be surprised to discover that they can see their best selves reflected in your eyes.

PART III

BEING A FRIEND

CHAPTER 7

DINA
EMBARKING UPON
NEW RELATIONSHIPS

The Biblical Story

Dina, the only daughter of Leah and Jacob, went out to visit the women of the land. Shechem, son of Hamor the Hivite, prince of the land called Shechem, saw her and took her and lay with her by force. Being strongly drawn to Dina, daughter of Jacob, and in love with her, he spoke to her tenderly. So Shechem said to his father, "Get me this girl as a wife."

Jacob had heard that Shechem had defiled his daughter Dina; but since his sons were in the field with his cattle, Jacob kept silent until they came home. Then Shechem's father, Hamor, came out to Jacob to speak to him.

Meanwhile, Jacob's sons, having heard the news, came in from the field. They were distressed and very upset because Shechem had committed a disgrace in Israel by lying with Jacob's daughter—a thing not done. Hamor spoke, saying, "My son Shechem so longs for your daughter. Please give her to him in marriage. Intermarry with us: give us your daughters and take our daughters for yourselves."

Jacob's sons answered Shechem and his father, Hamor, deceitfully because he had defiled their sister Dina, and said to them, "Only on this condition will we agree with you: that you will become like us by having every male among you circumcised." On the third day, when they were in pain, Simeon and Levi, two of Jacob's sons, brothers of Dina, took their swords, came upon the city without being harmed, and killed all the males. They killed Hamor and Shechem with their swords and took Dina out of Shechem's house and went away.

Jacob said to Simeon and Levi, "You have made trouble for me, making me odious among the inhabitants of the land."
But they answered, "Should our sister be treated like a whore?"
—Adapted from Genesis 34:1–31

Dina's Own Story

The tent Dina shared with her mother, Leah, was hot and airless. These were the days of late summer, and she could tolerate being inside only during the night or when escaping the midday sun. If her brothers could control her totally, they would keep her in the tent all the time, so anxious were they that she would steal away and be violated when they left the camp. "You'll be treated as if you were meat," they warned her, "swooped down upon by birds of prey."

Leah offered her daughter no sympathy: "It is our way: women stay home. Listen to your brothers. They are protecting you because they love you."

Only Jacob, her father, sometimes hinted that he understood how Dina felt, trapped and entombed. Standing just outside the doorway of her tent, she watched the boys go out into the fields. "The world will come to you," he promised, pulling at her braids. "Be patient. Destiny will come to you."

No one came, not even the young women of Shechem, who surely were just down the hill, so close Dina could hear their voices. They, too, must have been constrained by their fathers and brothers. "Why can't you bless my going out," Dina asked her father, "just as you bless my staying in?" He laughed, thinking Dina understood.

Dina refused to understand. As a girl, she had been patient. She had finally grown into the body of a young woman and she felt like a cucumber, pickled in brine for some holiday season many moons ahead.

Admittedly, as much as she desired to step out to meet the women of Shechem, she didn't know *how* to leave home, or how to open a conversation with someone outside the family. Her brothers knew because they had so much practice. They went out, and in their dealings, they had became worldly men. She stayed in and simply didn't become.

Leaning against her tent, Dina twisted her spindle, remembering that when her family had traveled from Mahanaim to Seir to Paddan-aram and then to Shechem in the land of Canaan, she dared herself to wander off at each stopping place. But she hadn't the courage to catch the attention of strangers unrelated to her by blood, even when they were but one or two shepherd girls filling flasks at their wells.

That night when her brothers returned, they loudly assembled at a fire in front of Jacob's tent with stories to tell. Dina listened with pleasure. She heard of Judah's dealings with the rough-and-tumble sheepshearers in Timnah, Zebulun's incredulous tales of spying ships floating along the sea, Asher's stories of trading for dainty pastries from the bakers of Shechem, Joseph's sightings of wild harts, ibexes, and—he must have dreamed this one up, she thought—lions. When the new stories were exhausted, they retold their old ones, augmenting details, inventing dialogue where there was none before. Each brother showed off his prowess for forging smart connections that would better establish the family in their new surroundings. Jacob had set the standard in his clan for negotiations. For just a hundred *kesitahs* and the promise of good will, he had convinced Hamor, the chief of Shechem, to sell him the parcel of land on which their tents were now pitched.

Dina tried to imagine having a story of her own to tell, of connections she had made that could widen their world. Her story would make her brothers lean forward with curiosity and jealousy, their elbows on their knees, their faces lit orange by the fire.

What if it were she, and not her father, who had encountered angels of God ascending and descending a ladder? She would have learned the name of each angel. She would have held on to their wings, climbed on their backs, and followed them homeward—and then she'd reciprocate, inviting them to her home. If she could only meet people outside her world, hear their languages, eat their foods, shop for red ribbon in their bazaars, wear their clothes, style her hair as they did. She would make a friend, who would reach for her hand, pull her aside, and say, "I have a secret, and I'm telling only you, and you can't tell a soul." Her friend would trust her with her tears. Dina would touch her friend's disheveled hair, push it back from her face, and know what to say.

But she was stuck, going nowhere. Even if she made offerings day and night at her father's altar to his god El-Elohei-Yisrael, she'd still be restrained by the sameness of every day. Nothing, nothing would ever happen to her that she couldn't anticipate. How was her destiny going to unfold if she could hardly move two steps away from her tent? The goats she tended had greater freedom to roam.

She would step out. Tomorrow morning, at sunrise.

Dina stayed up all night baking cakes for the Queen of Heaven. She would understand. She would give Dina courage to meet the women of Shechem. Dina baked the wheat cakes her mother and aunts usually prepared. Then she mixed up batters of her own for raisin cakes, cumin cakes, cakes of slivered, dried apricots spun out like a wheel. Making them, she imagined explaining to a new friend how she did it. She held out her arms in worship as the cakes rose, her arms and legs posed like inverted triangles, connected tip to tip. She drew in strength from the powers of heaven and earth, and as she did this, she practiced how she would tell her friend how she and the women of the family worshipped the Queen of Heaven when the men turned their backs. She and her friend would share songs and planting skills, ways to make plant dyes and turn hides into cloth, ways to calm and comfort the sick with herbs and compresses, strategies to heal a goat who was slow to give milk or a chicken that would not lay eggs. Relying on each other and sharing resources, they could become two peoples inhabiting the same land in peace.

Dina kept the oven fired, and slid the small cakes in on a wooden pallet. When they were ready, she let them cool on a stone shelf. Before morning, she arranged some of the cakes in a circle, and to this offering she added slowly burning myrrh. Brushing away the crumbs—and with them, any hesitations she held—she wrapped up the remaining cakes. She put the cakes into her pack, and added gifts of pistachio nuts and almonds she had filched from Aunt Rachel's storage jars.

With her pack over her shoulder and a branch as her walking stick, Dina stepped out. Dust clung to the dew that had formed on her sandals. She stepped beyond constraints, beyond borders, beyond desperation. She would begin by making a friend. One friend, a friend who knew her, maybe as well or better than she knew herself.

Dina walked toward the exotic, high-pitched, nasal chants of the young women of Shechem. Were these their morning prayers? She loped as if she had sprouted wings, moving across windflowers and sunburned grasses toward their voices, toward the sound of the bells and drums they played. Dina allowed herself to imagine they sang a welcome song in her honor.

The lizards in Dina's path scattered. She slowed her pace to catch her breath. In measured steps over a landscape of unfamiliar stones and a path of young fig trees beginning to bear their first tiniest nubs of green fruits, Dina rehearsed what she would say when she arrived. "I am called Dina, daughter of Leah and Jacob?" her voice raising in inflection, as if her identity were a question. And until now, it had been. She walked forward. She could taste friendship and the possibilities it held; it was like sweet tea.

Dina Speaks to Us

Dina is the seventh child of Leah, her only daughter, and the only sister of twelve brothers, some prone to violence (these are the same brothers who would cast their youngest brother, Joseph, into a pit and sell him into slavery). Dina, hungry for female friends her own age, had long tired of being in the company of older women, all of whom had children with her father: her aunt Rachel, the concubines Bilhah and Zilpah, and her mother, Leah. And so Dina stepped out.

According to the narrative we have received from the Bible, our heroine's choice to journey into an unknown world meets with immediate disaster. She is raped by a prince's son, Shechem, and held captive in his family's compound. Shechem claims he loves her and begs his father to make a betrothal acceptable to Dina's family.

There are biblical scholars, such as Tikva Frymer-Kensky, author of *Reading the Women of the Bible: A New Interpretation of Their Stories*, whose close analysis of the text leads us to question if Dina was indeed raped. Perhaps what happened was that she chose to engage in sexual relations without the consent of the men of her tribe who controlled access to her and saw that control as a sign of their own power. Perhaps there was mutual attraction between Dina and her prince, love at first sight that was interpreted by her brothers as rape. Whatever the nature of her initial encounter with Shechem, Dina may have come to love him and may have preferred to stay with him and be part of his household. (This story is convincingly told by Anita Diamant in her novel *The Red Tent*.)

Ancient legends that embroider upon this story teach that Dina's going out to meet the locals was audacious and wanton, and hence, she invited the rape. They say she was the seductive one, provoking Shechem's interest. They teach that it's dangerous for women to venture out in the world, because consciously or not, they incite men to violence. (Curious, isn't it, that the solution isn't to keep men under wraps, instead of women?)

There is no question that Dina was curious about her environment, and that curiosity led to complications. (Isn't that the heroic story we tell about the great European explorers and about Lewis and Clark?) But Dina's story did not have to end as it did, in death and violence. Negotiation did ensue between the fathers to resolve the situation harmoniously. The negotiations would have stabilized Dina's relationship with Shechem and would have paved the way for alliances between the two tribes. Her lover and his father were ready to meet Dina's people and to make compromises. They went so far as to circumcise all the males of Hamor's community to make amends. Dina's brothers, however, could not accept reconciliation. They feigned acquiescence, negotiating in bad faith, then killed the men living in Shechem. When we see Dina a last time, her brothers are "rescuing" her from the house of Shechem.

From the moment Dina steps out, she is no longer an active agent in our story and her choices or motivations no longer spin the plot. She becomes a passive object, acted upon by others, denied a say about her fate and well-being. We never hear from her again, never see her acting autonomously.

Dina is not the only biblical woman who went out to seek relationships, ignoring the boundaries usually imposed by her culture and her family. A number of other such women risked stepping out, but in contrast to Dina's story, which ends tragically, their stories have felicitous endings. There is Tamar, who steps out of her father's tent so she can conceive the child that is rightfully hers and, in doing so, teaches her father-in-law a lesson about ethics. There is Esther, who steps away from her guardian Mordechai and enters the palace, marries the king, and negotiates for the safety of her people. And there is Ruth, the young widow who steps away from her homeland of Moab and journeys to Bethlehem with her mother-in-law. Taking on a new faith and culture, she takes care of her mother-in-law and continues the line that will lead to King David.

These are not cautionary tales, but tales of heroic women making important national contributions. From such stories you could easily deduce that stepping outside the boundaries of familiar places and connecting with new people allows new worlds to open up. Interestingly, in all these scenarios, the woman who steps out lacks the father, brother, or husband who would hold her back. From a literary perspective, the unfettered heroine makes a far more engaging character, because she has agency. She can do interesting things and make choices. When she faces danger, she is not considered foolhardy, but brave. She is able to be transformed by her experiences.

This explains why heroines who are orphaned or abandoned by their parents are common figures in the children's books girls so adore. Consider Pippi Longstocking, Dorothy in *The Wizard of Oz*, or the Little Princess. Even Nancy Drew is motherless. Absent constraining parents, the heroine is positioned for adventure and growth. A most endearing heroine, Meg in Madeleine L'Engle's *A Wrinkle in Time*, can go off on a journey of self-discovery and confidence building into a sci-fi, four-dimensional world only because her scientist father has disappeared and her absentminded scientist mother is too distracted to notice her daughter has gone off. This frees Meg to muster up the courage to find her father. Otherwise, Meg would still be home, a well-protected, self-conscious adolescent with her nose in a book, unaware that she could, by forging the right alliances and taking risks, successfully fight against evil in the world.

But Dina is neither orphaned nor abandoned, and this makes her stepping out problematic. She has multiple mother figures, a father, and a flock of brothers. The women, by habit, constrain her as they have been constrained. The men define their honor, virility, and capital by their capacity to protect the virgin in their midst. (This remains the case in villages in southeastern Turkey, where "honor killings" take place when fathers and brothers take vengeance when unmarried women in their clan have been made pregnant, through rape or consensual sex.) The men of Dina's tribe would release her only when they were ready to make an agreeable marriage arrangement, transferring her, like property, into the care of another man.

If Dina's story had not ended violently with abuse and revenge, we'd have been better able to see the positive gesture that is Dina's hallmark, her stepping out. That gesture, her legacy to us, is her willingness to move beyond familiar relationships in safe, cozy settings and forge new bonds on unfamiliar turf. Dina had gumption. That may explain why, despite the awful turn of her story, her name is so often given to daughters.

Dina encourages us to step out and form relationships with unfamiliar people. Friendship, she tells us, can repair distances and acrimony between peoples who fear each other's distinctiveness.

In one medieval commentary, Dina is obediently ensconced in her tent and is lured outside only because Shechem has sent girls playing on timbrels to entice her with their music. Had she not been tricked, the teller wants to assure us, Dina, daughter of the venerated Jacob, would have stayed home like a good girl. We can read this medieval elaboration differently. Dina is *not* tricked by the music other women are playing. Instead, she has the gift of being able to hear the music of new relationships and ideas and having the gumption to move toward them.

Dina comes to tell us that just because her story of stepping out ended poorly, we must continue to be enticed by the music of otherness and risk stepping out. We must meet people who are different from us, people who might not like us at first, people who rattle us and leave us unbalanced. Most important, we should defy those who stand in the way of our taking risks in relationships. As my friend bioethicist Adrienne Asch once said, "Without intimacy, I'm not sure it's worth living in this world."

Dina tells us not to be seduced—not by predictable relationships, not by befriending the same kinds of people over and over. She urges us to overcome our mistrust and wariness of others who are different from ourselves. Try, at least, to build bridges. Risk intimacy; risk revealing too much, too soon about oneself to a new friend. Handle the discomfort of hearing more about a new friend than we are ready to learn. Enter a social situation that makes us shift our feet from side to side and stuff our hands in our pockets. Sidestep those who wish to keep us safe at all costs, even with the best of intentions. They rob us of being fully expansive, and they rob the world of our touch.

It is too risky, Dina teaches, for us to remain safe in our own tents. The global implications are obvious. We need to journey across our thresholds toward one another—with or without roadmaps—and there, at the crossroads where we happen to meet, we might break bread.

Embracing the Gift of Dina

When you step out to meet new people and make courageous connections, as Dina did, remember that this is a holy act. As you cross the threshold of your home and move toward bold or risky encounters that hold promise, invoke the angels of peace (*shalom*, in Hebrew, or *salaam*, in Arabic). Take the angels with you for companionship and courage as you leave the familiar and open yourself up to others.

Beacon the angels of peace that will accompany you by lighting candles in their honor and by offering words of welcome, such as these:

Welcome among us, messengers of peace.
Come in peace,
Bless us with peace,
And lead us in peace,
As we step out in your presence.
May we be blessed as we step out, and may we be blessed as we
    return.

You might also prepare your own homemade set of "angel cards." Decorate index cards with a miniature collage, each one representing a different angelic trait. These traits may include honesty, integrity, inspiration, joy, compassion, wholeness, curiosity, wisdom, imagination, social change, knowledge, cooperation, faith, praise, commitment, strength, order, remembrance, forgiveness, trust, openness, wonder, or serenity. In our home (we have various sets of angel cards created by my daughters and my students), our practice is for each person to select an angel card at random from the box we keep them in. We try to imagine that this angel will give us special guidance and strength all week long. (If we don't like the one we first pick, we get to try again—and again, if we wish.) When we do this together, as a family or with friends, we try to explain how the angelic trait we have chosen is a particularly relevant companion for us, given what's going at that moment in our lives.

CHAPTER 8

JEPHTHAH'S DAUGHTER
BEING THERE FOR FRIENDS

The Biblical Story

Jephthah was an able warrior. His father was Gilead; his mother was a prostitute. Gilead's other sons by his wife drove Jephthah out; he fled from his brothers. Outlaws gathered about him and he went raiding with these empty men. When the Ammonites attacked Israel, the elders of Gilead went to bring Jephthah back: "Be our chief so we can fight the Ammonites." Jephthah replied, "You hated me and drove me out. Now you come back to me when you are in trouble?" The elders promised, "As God is our witness, if you come with us and fight, you shall be our commander." Jephthah went with the elders of Gilead, and the people made him their commander in chief. And Jephthah repeated the terms of their agreement before God at Mizpah.

The spirit of the Lord was with Jephthah as he marched into battle. He made this vow to God: "If you deliver the Ammonites into my hands, then I will offer whoever comes out the door of my house to meet me upon my safe return as a burnt offering to God." Jephthah attacked the Ammonites and was victorious.

When he arrived at his home in Mizpah it was his daughter, his only child, who came out to meet him with timbrel and dance. Upon seeing her, he tore his clothes. "Alas, daughter, how you have brought me to the depths; what trouble you have caused me. For I have spoken a vow to God and I cannot take back my words."

"Father," she said, "you have made a vow to God. You must keep it, doing to me what you have vowed, as God made you successful in defeat-

ing your enemies." Moreover, she said to him, "Do this for me: grant me
two months, and I shall spend that time with my women friends. I will
go with them to the hills to cry, I and my friends, for my lost youth."

"Go" he replied. He let her go for two months, and she and her women
friends cried together in the hills. After two months, she returned to her
father, and he sacrificed her as he had vowed. She had never slept with a
man. It became the custom for the young women of Israel to go out for
four days every year to lament Jephthah's daughter.

—Adapted from Judges 11:1–11, 29–40

Jephthah's Daughter's Own Story

On the morning the young women of Mizpah had seen their fathers
ride off to battle (not again—would they ever stop leaving?), they
returned to sit together in Sheilah's house. They had thought to take
the morning meal together and bake flat breads on the stone but found
themselves not hungry at all.

This time they felt a deep foreboding, Sheilah especially. She was the
daughter of Jephthah, who had been called to command this battle. She
was the tallest of the friends, the most robust, the one who could always
push her friends to sustain themselves and stay strong. On this morning, she felt too distracted to initiate the baking. She just heated water
on the fire and made an infusion of dried mint. They warmed themselves until the sun rose by holding their clay cups in both hands and
sitting close together.

Anat, Ya'irah, Na'amah, and Sheilah had been friends since their
baby days when their mothers nursed side by side. Inseparable, they
called each other "sisters in life, forever, ever." Daughters of soldiers of
the Gilead community, they had grown up seeing fathers go off to battle, and they became skilled readers of their fathers' moods. From the
way he packed his gear to the way he readied himself to leave, a girl
could discern her father's measure of courage or terror. In the clench
of his embrace, she would know his resolve or sense his trembling.
Upon his return, she could tell if he would be terrorized by nightmares
of swords.

Sheila could tell from her father's precision as he prepared the blankets for his horse that more was at stake for him this time than ever before. "How will it end?" asked Anat, birdlike and fidgety, who absorbed herself in the dramatic possibilities any outcome might personally afford her. "Will I be dancing toward my father with garlands in my hair, welcoming him home as the victor, singing 'I will praise You, Lord, with all my heart; I will rejoice, for you destroy the wicked, the enemy is no more'? Or will I be darkening my house and my heart forever, covering myself in sackcloth, lowering myself to the floor in mourning, chanting, 'How long, my God, will you ignore me forever? How long will you hide your face from me?'"

"There isn't a flower here the horses haven't trampled on," Anat continued. "We'll have to go up to the hills to make any decent garlands."

"Your life could unfold either way," said Ya'irah, weary of it all and wearied of Anat's attempts to make her own role in the warfare seem significant when young women were so clearly marginal. Of the friends, Ya'irah was the only one still waiting for her body to mature, but her soul had always been an old one. She did not tolerate drama for its own sake. "You never know if your father will return or not. There is nothing a girl can do but wait. My mother insists I *can* do something—I can pray and hold the family together—but I'm done with that. It feels like all I'm doing is keeping busy, distracting myself as I twist my spindle, affirming that I make no difference at all."

Was it not possible, wondered bubbly Na'amah, ever the idealist, that one day the girls and women could welcome their fathers home for good? The women would praise God: "See what the Lord has done. He puts a stop to war throughout the world, breaking the bow, snapping the spear, consigning the wagons of war to the flames." This is exactly what she said each time the fathers departed for battle. As she started chanting her verses, Anat and Sheilah chimed in with her, their voices mimicking the old granny who circled the village also chanting these words each morning and evening.

"Enough, Na'amah, of the lovely words," said Ya'irah. "They are the fantasies of women's prayers. War entices men. In the battlefield, they give birth to a part of themselves they'd otherwise never know. If they didn't have real enemies, they'd invent them."

Sheilah believed Ya'irah was right about peace being women's fantasy. She pictured herself with strings in her hand, fashioning Jephthah's broken bow into a harp. She imagined his unfocussed face: Without an enemy to destroy, he could find no purpose. Without an enemy, how would he release his explosive anger? If he could no longer kill the enemy who threatened him, might he turn even more violently on those he loved?

Sheilah thought she might finally confide in her friends about her father's rage that frequently exploded out of nowhere. Her mother witnessed it, though she said nothing—she cowered, staying away until he calmed. Then she plied him with heavy foods that put him to sleep. For sure, the soldiers under his command had to have witnessed his rages. Maybe what made him a monster at home, coupled with a gift for devious strategy, made him a star in the battlefield.

Sheilah still hesitated to speak of her father's rages to her friends. It wasn't all of who he was, she rationalized each time; it came of his harsh childhood, being ostracized by his brothers. Why talk of something you couldn't change?

She had never kept anything from her "sisters in life" but this. Now, there was a new troubling confidence she felt she had to withhold from her friends. It was what she had overheard outside her window—or at least thought she had overheard—in the moments before the men rode down from Mizpah. Had she been dreaming? Unlikely, as she remembered leaning up against her cool window as the men gathered before dawn. There was the sound of her father's voice, but she could not make out all his words: "I . . . this vow. . . . If I am victorious . . . sacrifice the first soul . . ."

What was he saying? Unthinkable, banish the thought. A nightmare, a conversation misheard, taken out of context.

Within days, the time feeling longer than it actually was, the fathers returned home from war triumphant. The sound of their singing was even louder than the pounding of their horses. The daughters scurried to prepare themselves to dance, each about to perform first for her own father. They would fall into their fathers' arms, pull them indoors, feed them, and cushion them with softness. They would then assemble as a group to perform the traditional "welcoming home the warrior" dance for all the soldiers, first honoring their fathers with a warm, loving gaze, then taking surreptitious glances at the young single men who might catch their eyes.

On her head, Sheilah placed the garland of cyclamen and poppies she had been preparing as she wandered in the low hills alone earlier that day, pondering the words her father had spoken before he departed. From her window she now saw her father sitting on his horse. He did not move to dismount. Her friends' fathers and the young men who had gone with them in battle waited on their stilled horses behind him. They looked downward, as if they had come to honor a fallen comrade. The singing had stopped. She didn't understand. Why were they there and not going first to be received by their own families?

She breathed in slowly. She danced out her door, but not into her father's arms. Into his rage. He howled. She felt as if his spear had gone right through her. "It's all your fault," he stormed. "You stupid, stupid girl, whatever were you thinking? Look what you made me do!"

"What have I done?" she demanded, knowing she had done nothing at all but act in the proper way and display the proper sentiments.

Sheilah waited for someone, anyone, to speak. The soldiers were silent. The mothers and the elders who had crept out of their houses were silent. There was no voice of protest, only the screams of her girl-friends. Their mothers took no chances and pushed them back into their own homes, forbidding them to come out, lest Jephthah's vow be contagious.

Hearing her father's explanation, Sheilah knew she was to die. This was the will of her father and apparently the will of the village and of God. She went silent, but loudly so. She refused to rage against death with an anger that mirrored her father's.

Her decision was clear and immediate. If she had but days to live, she would embrace the familiar blessings of this life, celebrating them with her friends, the ones who loved her best and knew her best. This would be her remonstration.

"I will not die yet," Sheilah told her father, and walked past him, and past all the soldiers who would not meet her gaze. She went from door to door, gathering her "sisters in life, forever, ever," pulling them out of their houses despite their mothers' protests, telling them they should prepare to go with her to the hills. "We will live together, cook, make fires, watch animals, and sleep side by side," she told Ya'irah, then Anat, then Na'amah. "We will celebrate our being grown women."

"What are we going to do?" they wanted to know when they assembled. They were ashamed they had no ideas of their own.

"If I thought there was something any of you could do to save my life, I would ask you. But there is nothing to be done, and I will not spend my last days grasping at straws. You will help me uphold my dignity. Live together with me in the hills. Imagine a perfect world with me, one day after another." She bade Anat, Ya'irah, and Na'amah to sing their old song, "How good it is when sisters dwell together." They sang this to her, placing the garlands they had woven for their fathers at her feet.

They left as soon as they could gather up their supplies. What did they do in the hills for two months? None of the young women would ever say when they returned. But they did declare that four days of memorial would be kept each year for their friend. The story has come down that they spent their time lamenting that Sheilah would end her life without ever knowing the pleasure of lying with a man or having a child. When Anat, Ya'irah, and Na'amah were grandmothers and heard that this was the story being told, they laughed. "Wouldn't you know!" they said. "We did nothing of the sort."

Jephthah's Daughter Speaks to Us

Of all the stories in the Bible concerning women, the one about Jephthah's daughter is perhaps the most troubling. The first time I read it, I was an adult, and I was shocked that no teacher had ever brought it to my attention, as if it were pornography (and in some ways, perhaps it is). Each time I read it I am startled afresh. Horrified, I ask myself how any society could have allowed this to happen.

When the story is taught nowadays, it is frequently used to bring attention to the plight of women who are abused, physically or psychologically. It is taught to remind women to speak up about any abuse they have endured and to protect themselves.

The story of Jepthah's daughter is also used to remind us how important it is to tell women's stories. While we do not know what happened when the young women spent two months together in the hills, we do know that their descendants took four full days each year just to tell the story.

These are huge insights for our time, especially in communities slow to recognize the abuse and domestic violence in their midst, let alone to address it. Because these aspects of Jephthah's daughter's story have been well taught in our time, I feel free to turn to a different wisdom that Jephthah's daughter imparts to us. This insight comes at the very end of her story, like a coda. She wants us to understand there are two different ways a friend can be helpful: by offering to repair her problem, and by bearing witness.

First we must enter the core of the story. Jephthah, a warrior who came from the family of Gilead, had no status in his family and no claim to inheritance, for he, unlike his brothers, was the son of a prostitute. His brothers drove him out of town and turned to him only when they needed his soldiering skills to fight against the Ammonites. The brothers struck a deal: if Jephthah was successful in conquering the enemy, they would make him head of the Gileads. The spirit of God was with Jephthah as he went into battle, but Jephthah craved more assurance and made a deal with God in the form of a sacred vow. If successful in battle, he would sacrifice whomever chanced to come out his door first to meet him upon his return. Not one soldier witnessing the vow said, "It's the people you love who walk out the door to greet you." No one who heard him cautioned him to recall, "Our God abhors human sacrifice."

Jephthah was successful in battle, and we readers cringe, anticipating what's to come. In those days, women greeted heroic warriors with dances and the music of timbrels. His daughter (nameless in the Bible, but called Sheilah in some of the ancient legends), his only child, emerged from their house to greet him, as he knew she would. Jephthah tore his clothes and began to mourn. Defying logic but not human nature, he blamed *her*, saying, "How could you have done this to me?"

There was no last-minute rescue, no lamb provided by God, no communal elders who stood between a father and his vow in order to protect a vulnerable person in their midst. Outrageous, but how very human not to protest the social order when a more vulnerable member of a society is threatened. Sheilah, in an act of enormous piety and, simultaneously, of social critique, insisted that her father keep his vow. But before she could be sacrificed (we assume she was put to death, but some legends imagine she may have spent her life dedicated to temple service), she obliged her father to sanction the two months she and her women friends would spend together in the hills. It's interesting to note that going away together for that purpose may have been something women had never before done.

Then we have the coda, the scene of women lamenting together on a hillside. How much the women had to lament. That a father could honor his commitments to God before he honored his commitments to his family. That military victory could be placed over the peacefulness of one's home, over life itself. That God did not stop the violence of men against women.

The coda is a spiritual journey of sorts. In the archetypal spiritual journey, an individual goes off alone to a high place, such as a mountain, for illumination or self-purification. What makes the story of Jephthah's daughter distinctive is that at the moment of crisis, when a community's moral system has proven flawed, when the way people relate to God and each other has gone off course, a group of women make a spiritual journey together. They, who have witnessed all that has gone wrong in their society, take time out to create the story that will offer testimony—and perhaps create the building blocks for a new civilization. One is reminded of those who came off the ark with Noah. How much evil they had seen, how much destruction, and after forty days apart from their society, they had a testimony to bear and a new world to create.

In the presence of her friends, Sheilah did not lament the past. She did not complain about things she could not change. She mourned the loss of a future she anticipated: love, children, the joys and sorrows of everyday life that she took for granted.

The women cared for their friend in the time they had together, and they promised they would remember and retell her story. There was love on those hills, the healing love of friendship. As Lauren Slater has written, it was a place filled with "the lovely and mysterious alchemy that comprises the cords between people, the cords that soothe some terrors and help us heal."[1]

Would that Sheilah's women friends had been socially and politically powerful enough to spend their time in the hills not lamenting but organizing, finding a way to avert their friend's destiny. Would that they could have protested Jephthah's vow, obliging him to find a way to thank God for victory other than by murdering his daughter. But none of them alone, and not even all of them together, were able to find a way for their friend to rebel against her world or to transform it.

In the absence of a solution, Sheilah spent her last days in the rich and loving presence of her friends. We must not say that these days were of no meaning because they did nothing to change her fate. Perhaps Sheilah, when thinking about these days of connectedness, could claim, again in Slater's words, "I believe in a place, somewhere in the air, where myself and your self might meet, merging in what we might learn to call, at least for a moment, love."[2]

Sheilah knew precisely how she wanted her friends to be present for her. She had not invited them to change her life but to do what friends can do when a situation cannot be rectified, changed, or fixed. They witnessed. They heard her pain. The experience of being fully present moved them so much that they repeated the story for generations.

Sheilah and her friends teach us that when a friend is in crisis (or, to take it down a notch, even if she's just "in a pickle"), there are two constructive ways to respond. One response is *to repair*. You know your friend well enough to understand what's broken in her life, and you encourage her to see the problem (especially if she lacks the perspective to do so) and to fix it. If she can't fix the problem herself, you give her the resources she needs or help her to find them. If your support, advice, and encouragement still don't lead her to fix what's broken, you roll up your sleeves and do what's needed to be done. If your friend is endangered, physically or psychologically, you call for help or you go right over and take care of her yourself or get her to the emergency room. If the crisis your friend is experiencing is a problem that many women deal with, one that is systemic and not an isolated personal event, such as sexual harassment at work or a hiring practice that discriminates against women, you get her permission to call around or go online and help connect her to others who have dealt effectively with this problem. If you need to organize locally to address the problem—say, your friend is dealing with domestic violence and there is no shelter in your community she could go to—you ask her to permit you to put your organizing skills to work. You strategize about how to make changes, you gain the support of others who want to address the problem, and you work collectively to do what needs to be done.

The alternative response is *to witness*. You hear what's happening in your friend's life. You take in all of the details; you listen to her whole life story if need be. You offer yourself as a sounding board, as a font of moral support. You resist saying, "I know just how you feel," because in fact, you know you do not. You resist saying, "The same exact thing happened to me" because even if it did, even if your own situation could not have been more similar, it is not *your* experience of the situation that is at stake right now, but your friend's very separate and distinct experience. For certain, you don't tell her, "The same thing happened to someone I know, and it was even worse!"

Instead, you acknowledge that while your friend may have every reason to take on the world and fight, you respect her decision if she chooses not to. You don't take up her cause in her stead. You acknowledge some things can't be fixed and that rotten stuff does happen. You do not offer solutions or escapes, though you certainly make it known that should assistance of any kind be needed, you are available. If there's a crisis that passes and then returns again, you play the role of historian, reminding your friend, "We have a pattern here."

At times, bearing witness is what our friends genuinely need us to do. Doing so, however, may not always feel rewarding. When you call and say, "I'm just checking in to hear how things are," and you don't hear progress, it may feel as if you are letting your friend down, failing to step up and become actively involved in the way friends are supposed to. It may even feel as if she were letting you down, because she is not giving you the opportunity to come through as her friend when she is in need. At the very least, you may feel frustrated. (I know my husband, like many who are good problem solvers, gets frustrated when I tell him that when I complain or vent, I'm *not* asking for him to fix what's wrong—I just want him to listen.)

How are we to know when to repair and when to bear witness? Jephthah's daughter and her friends teach us this: unless a friend is so fragile or vulnerable that she cannot make a decision for herself, and unless her life is in danger, the choice is not ours to make. Respectfully, we must give it over to our friend, and honor her choice and her autonomy in doing so.

Embracing the Gift of Jephthah's Daughter

To perform the ritual of friendship of Jephthah's daughter, ask your friend who seems to need your help to specify exactly how she would like you to support her when she has a problem, by repairing or by witnessing. Instead of letting things fall into place "naturally," responding to each other out of habit, or assuming you simply *know* what your friend wants, ask her, "What do you wish me to do?" (Obviously, you're not going to give your friend the choice if you believe your friend is in physical or psychological danger.)

You then abide by your friend's decision. Maybe your friend does indeed want you to be the fixer, even the miracle worker. Maybe your efforts will be treated with great gratitude. You may even be asked to get more actively involved than you anticipated.

But she might prefer for you to stand by and do what may feel to you like doing nothing. This may make you uncomfortable, because you would rather act. But being fully present for a friend is not doing nothing. It's another way of being involved and caring.

After a time, continue to support your friend by revisiting your earlier conversation. Does she still want you to support her in the particular manner she has requested? She may have changed her mind, or you may have discovered you are unable to fill the role you have been asked to play.

The tokens we give friends often symbolize our efforts to help them. When we give a gift certificate for a massage or a miniature Zen sand garden to a stressed-out friend, or a night out at a restaurant for the friend who has too many burdens and too few resources, we are sending a message: "You have a problem and I have come to help you with my solution." Other gifts represent our effort to bear witness: a photograph, a phone card, stationery. The presents we give should be the ones that correspond to a friend's choice for assistance.

As a sign that you and your friend are observing the ritual of Jephthah's daughter, tie a red ribbon onto each other's wrists. With roots in the Bible, wearing a red ribbon remains a powerful custom in many cultures and is enjoying a renewal these days. The red ribbon is a sign of keeping away the evil eye—that is, not just the malevolent thought of those who are jealous but all sources of danger that might befall us, our loved ones, and those outside our circles whom we embrace. The red ribbon you both wear is a sign that your friendship is a source of strength.

NAOMI AND RUTH
REVISING MOTHER-DAUGHTER RELATIONSHIPS

The Biblical Story

There was a famine in the land and a man of Bethlehem in Judah, Elim-elech, went with his wife and two sons to reside in the land of Moab. Elim-elech, Naomi's husband, died, and she was left with her two sons, Mahlon and Chilion. They married Moabite women named Orpah and Ruth and they lived there about ten years. Then Mahlon and Chilion also died: the woman was left without her two sons and without her husband.

Naomi started to return to Bethlehem with her daughters-in-law, for she had heard that the Lord had taken note of the people and given them food. Accompanied by her two daughters-in-law, she left the place she had been living in and they set out on their way back to the land of Judah.

But Naomi said to her two daughters-in-law, "Turn back, each of you, to your mother's house. May the Lord deal kindly with you, just as you have dealt with the dead and with me. May the Lord grant that each of you find security in the house of a husband. She kissed them farewell. They broke into tears and said, "No, we will return with you to your people."

But Naomi replied, "Turn back, my daughters, and go your own way. Can I give birth to sons who might become husbands for you? Oh no, my daughters. My lot is far bitterer than yours, for the Lord has turned against me."

They broke into tears again. Orpah kissed her mother-in-law good-bye, but Ruth clung to her. Naomi said, "Your sister-in-law has returned to her people and to her gods. Go, follow her."

Ruth replied, "Do not press me to leave you, to turn back and not fol-
low you. For wherever you go, I will go; wherever you lodge, I will lodge;
your people shall be my people and your God my God. Where you die I
will die, and there I will be buried. Thus and more may the Lord do to
me if anything but death parts me from you." When Naomi saw how
determined Ruth was to go with her, she ceased to argue with her, and the
two continued on until they reached Bethlehem.

—Adapted from Book of Ruth 1

Naomi and Ruth's Own Story

Nothing had turned out, Naomi reflected, as she and Elimelech had planned. Starting in their courtship, they discussed everything, holding the illusion that if they plotted out their lives in enough detail, they could avoid the missteps that befell those who lacked foresight. Their lives would unfold just so. There was the plan to live well in Bethlehem, to raise a family there and have the respect of their community. They would find their children excellent spouses from distinguished families of Bethlehem to provide them with grandchildren. They would grow old together, and the villagers would consult with them to resolve matters of business and disputes of love. Keen on independence, they would hire attendants to care for them in their elder years, just as their own parents had, to preserve their dignity. The thought of their own children wiping away crumbs of food from their mouths was unthinkable.

With the famine, every stitch of the planning had come undone. They were left with no way to survive in Bethlehem, let alone in the elegant style to which they were accustomed. What choice was there but to move with their two sons to Moab? Temporarily, of course. Settling into Moab and feeling so quickly comfortable there, watching saplings grow into trees and fields of sown barley become thick each year, how easy it was for them to push away the thought of returning to Bethlehem. Life back home in Bethlehem was allegedly not as harsh anymore, but it was still uncertain. After this Passover season they would return with the boys, or next year perhaps—for absolute sure, the next. But then years passed.

One day Elimelech, Naomi's beloved, the sustainer of her soul, collapsed dead in her arms as he held her in greeting at the end of the day. His weight pulled her down to the ground as if he desired to take her with him. Would that he had! Distant from her homeland, who could console Naomi in the familiar ways of her people? Losing Elimelech, living without him, had never been part of the plan, and without a plan, she felt lost, drowning in tears and emptiness. But after the months of mourning, she pulled herself together for the sake of her sons.

Mahlon and Chilion had become willowy, generous men. Perhaps if Elimelech had lived, he could have prevented them from falling in love with the young women of Moab. Naomi alone could not keep them away from the country girls who laughed at their jokes. Each fell in love with a Moabite girl, sisters as it happened, and married. Naomi had long bad-mouthed Moabite girls in the abstract: they were too pale, too thin; they masked their sweat with a smelly perfume and ate full knobs of raw garlic to stay healthy. "These are the kind of people you bring into your house as servants, not as family," she said behind their backs.

When Ruth and Orpah first came into Naomi's tent as daughters-in-law, Naomi was cold, keeping her distance even when they spoke. Ruth and Orpah both trusted that in time, they would each find a place for themselves in her heart. They consulted Naomi for advice continually, for their own mother, who had little feel for the raising of children, had taught them nothing. How much Naomi knew! You could ask her anything. How do you know when the meat in your stew is ready? How did you keep your husband, Elimelech, adoring you? What amulets and herbs help to conceive?

Naomi answered their questions in growing detail and came to enjoy dispensing advice each day. She demonstrated how to distill a perfume of rose petals as they did back in Bethlehem and how to roast the head of garlic before eating it. Ruth and Orpah were fascinated by Naomi's ways, the practices of this once-wondrous place she came from, this Bethlehem. They indulged her by listening to memories of a privileged childhood. Her tales became real to them, as did her stories of her people's exodus from Egypt, the bread of affliction they had carried, the pilgrimage feasts they now made, and her god. Ruth, in particular, learned to speak of Naomi's ancestors Abraham and Sarah as her own;

so present she could feel them watching her. She came to imagine the Holy One who protected Naomi's people guarding her own steps as well.

The sisters observed Naomi engaging with her sons in continuous talks about future plans: for crops, for the breeding of animals, for the new dwellings that would be built as her sons' households grew. Not that the future would always unfold as you planned it, but you still could work toward dreams and anticipate problems along with their solutions. From their own mother, the sisters had learned a more passive stance: there was fate, and you braced yourself and accepted it.

Soon, Naomi came to embrace Ruth and Orpah with the very same tenderness she extended to her sons. She would hold out her arms to Ruth and Orpah and say, "Come to me, come," and she would pull them into the softness of her large, round body.

One evening Ruth and Orpah both came running to Naomi, shrieking that their husbands had both died in their arms, just as suddenly as Elimelech had. Again, Naomi felt her life altogether unraveling.

Then the rains of spring failed to come. Naomi and her two sons' widows, each starved of love, were now literally starving. They could barely hold up a bucket of water or reach down and gather handfuls of wheat stalks around which hungry insects flew. There was no future left to imagine, only emptiness and the tears of widows.

At dawn, Naomi could see the small movements of her daughters-in-law, Ruth and Orpah, outside the tent that the three of them were sharing, as it had seemed foolhardy to lie alone at night and fear the howling of the wind. She had cried day and night after Elimelech's death. After her sons died, she went almost mute—could you cry if you could no longer feel? Naomi had grown accustomed to the sound of the daughters' wailing and muffled sobs, which, accompanying the wind, had become the background of their lives.

Now for the first time in weeks, she heard an unfamiliar morning sound. Was it a foreign language? The language of birds? Naomi emerged from the doorway of the tent to find Ruth and Orpah sitting on the parched ground with their legs stretched out and feet flexed upward. She was reminded of the stiff clay dolls the young women had brought from their homes and used to worship earlier on. In the scant light of early morning, the women had mixed up their sandals and ended up wearing one of her own and one of the other. This struck them as funny, so very funny, particularly as Ruth's feet were so small and Orpah's so much larger. They giggled and grew quiet only to erupt again in loud laughs. They sat their mother-in-law between them and each rested her head on one of Naomi's shoulders. Naomi pulled them both to her, and though her arms were so thin now, the daughters-in-law could still feel the security of her embrace.

If the women of Bethlehem could see Naomi, known for her stand-offish elegance, sitting here on the dirt, animated by the love of country girls, how shocked they would be. Naomi stuck her own legs out and flexed her feet upward and felt laughter rising up from her stomach.

"Mother," said Ruth, when the laughter slowed and grief began to flow back in, "I am so lonely. I'm starving and I don't even care."

"Well, at least my sandals match," Naomi offered, wiggling her feet until all three were laughing again.

The sight of shoes on their feet gave Naomi the idea of returning to Bethlehem with Ruth and Orpah. The idea arrived so fully formed that it was as if she was remembering a dream of the night before. She began to calculate. Stay in Moab and they would die of grief or hunger. This was not what Elimelech would have wanted. It did no honor to the memory of her sons if their wives were allowed to waste away. She was the matriarch and she would take charge of these girls who had become as dear to her as daughters. They were capable girls, and once they could find food again, they would be strong and useful. In Bethlehem, they would find a way to start over. They would do whatever they had to do: glean from the remains at the corners of the fields, find kinsmen who might see it in their hearts to shelter them.

"Look at me," thought Naomi as she pulled apart the rucksack she had begun to assemble and practiced wrapping her shawl for the desert crossing. "I'm planning again." But she quickly began to doubt herself. Did she think she could assure the safety of these two young women as they journeyed back; did she even remember the way? Could they make a fresh life for themselves among people who rightfully remembered her and Elimelech with bitterness for having abandoned them years ago when they might have stayed and endured the years of hardship together?

Though they had already struck their tent, Naomi called Ruth and Orpah to her. The plan was foolish; it was off. "Go back to your own mother's tent," Naomi commanded, "and she will take you in. Do this for me. Relieve me of being responsible for you."

Orpah, not wanting to be a burden, took Naomi at her word and returned home. But Ruth remained.

"Follow your sister," Naomi pleaded, but Ruth clung to her even as Naomi tried to drive her away. How could she leave Naomi? For Naomi had taught her so much—to plan, to dream of a future. Now Ruth opened herself to dreams no Moabite girl had ever imagined, dreams that Naomi could help her realize. Accompanying Naomi, Ruth would be like Abraham and Sarah, going forth to a land of blessing and promise. She and Naomi would care for each other and hold each other up along the way. They would give each other strength. She would commit herself to Naomi's god. No matter what, she and Naomi would have each other, all the history behind them, and whatever new was to unfold.

Together, the two women set off to begin life anew.

Naomi and Ruth Speak to Us

Talk about the Book of Ruth and in a moment we're talking about mothers and daughters: how Ruth puts herself at risk to look after Naomi, how Ruth clings to her; how they sustain each other through grief and regroup, forming a new kind of family; how Naomi teaches Ruth how to make her way among the barley planters of Bethlehem and get established in a complicated new world.

For the sake of accuracy, while we might choose to read the story of Naomi and Ruth's relationship as the Bible's paradigmatic mother and daughter, Naomi is, in fact, not Ruth's mother but her mother-in-law. Ruth, whom the story upholds as the paragon of loyalty, may be a widow, but she is not an orphan: she has a mother of her own in Moab. Though marriage took her out of her parents' clan and made her a surrogate daughter in the house of her in-laws, within her culture, the death of her husband gave her the opportunity to return to her own mother's house and seek help there. When commanded to do so by Naomi, Orpah does just this. Ruth does not. She selects Naomi as a surrogate mother, leaving her own mother behind. She commits herself to her mother-in-law as if she were her husband, taking the vow, "Whither thou goest, I shall go," so often spoken at weddings now.

What happened to honoring one's parents, the ethical ideal made clear enough in the Ten Commandments? Interestingly, many biblical narratives do not put being a mama's boy or a mama's girl over other virtues. How often biblical heroes leave their parents so they can go off into the world and achieve their own personal destiny, forming new alliances along the way. Abraham, for example, leaves his parents and journeys to a place of promise. In effect, God rewards him for cutting off his obligations to his family of birth. Would the story of Ruth have been told if she had told Naomi, "You're right. I think I'll stay home in Moab and go back to my mother's tent." For sure, there is no Book of Orpah.

Let us be clear here. The story of Ruth, a classical "how our hero was born" story, is remembered primarily because Ruth provides the womb through which the line of King David can flourish. Jews believe the Messiah will emerge from this line, and the Gospels of the New Testament consciously trace Jesus's lineage back to Ruth. I doubt Ruth's story would have been canonized had it been only about women's loyalties. Imagine: "Once upon a time, there was a young woman, Ruth, whose husband died. She left town with her mother-in-law, a widow as well, and took good care of her. Working together, pooling their resources, using cunning when necessary, the two of them got back on their feet." Not likely.

But when we choose to read the story focusing on the bond between Naomi and Ruth, they become guides, helping us to understand how relationships between mothers and daughters might be reframed over time.

Their unconventional relationship allows us to see that sometimes we may need to leave our own mothers behind—either physically or emotionally—and find new ones who will mother us better. This possibility is especially important for women who have lost their mothers or who are estranged from them. For most of us, we needn't literally disconnect from our mothers, though I understand for some people that is a life-giving choice. What we do need is to be able to leave behind old ways of relating to our mothers, to be creative and courageous enough to discontinue our destructive or inappropriate ways of interacting and sculpt new ones. It's the loyalty we have between us that propels us to do such hard work together.

The very mothers we love, the ones who want the best for us, can sometimes make us feel inept or insufficiently caring. Although they mean well, as they offer advice we haven't asked for, they might keep us from making our own mistakes and learning from them.

Naomi was the mother Ruth needed at this juncture in her life. Consider all that Naomi made possible for Ruth: she got her out of Moab, the land of her birth, where people were literally starving, where life had left Ruth stuck, hungry to test her mettle, to start out fresh after the death of her young husband. Naomi gave Ruth the opportunity to learn to live as a stranger among a different people with customs, even a god, unlike her own. Naomi opened the door for Ruth to learn the agricultural practices of the Judean barley farmers, to figure out how to ingratiate herself with the local aristocracy who could help her resettle.

Ultimately, Naomi gave Ruth a good many gifts we who are mothers might want to give our own daughters, or that we who are daughters might want to receive. Naomi gave Ruth the chance to break free, to be autonomous. In every way, Naomi made Ruth feel like a real daughter. She gave her responsibilities. She trusted in her. She cared for Ruth and allowed Ruth to care for her. She brought her into her family, helping her get established.

With equal intensity, Ruth took steps to make herself into a real daughter. She went with Naomi to her homeland to learn more about who she was: her language, customs, and food. She engaged in the life of Naomi's people, participating in their harvesting, even meeting the busybodies and giving them fodder for their gossip. Significantly, she embraced Naomi's god. She tried to learn how Naomi experienced holiness, and she learned how to enter that particular holy circle with her.

Naomi and Ruth are not telling us to abandon our birth mothers and find chummier ones, more in synch with the trajectory of our lives, more capable of opening doors. They are not telling us to become unavailable to our daughters when their expectations of our patience and generosity are unrealistic.

What Naomi and Ruth teach us is that both mothers and daughters can leave off the relational patterns we have inherited and create them anew, taking into consideration the people that we have become and the experiences that have shaped us.

We are not stuck, as we might believe, with the contours of our current relationship with our mother or our daughter. We can renegotiate the "rules of engagement" multiple times over the course of a lifetime. As daughters, we can find new parts of our mothers to cherish and fresh ways of seeing them as models. We can discover aspects of them that we will come to appreciate in different ways, especially as they need us more for their care. And we, too, can encourage our mothers to see us as being more competent than they had ever imagined.

As mothers, we can bid our daughters to relinquish the ways they used to see us and seek out those qualities we have that can lead them to bolder ways of being. We can help them to see that just as they keep changing and developing, we do too, and it would be worthwhile for us to encounter the people we are now, and not the ones frozen in memory.

The loyalty of Naomi and Ruth is not based on one terrific relationship that got sustained over years. They were two women, bound to each other over a long period. So many things changed in both their lives, and they continued to evolve with each shock and reshuffling. They were there for each other; they renegotiated the terms of their relationship. They gave each other power, encouragement, the insights of youth and age, more possibilities than either could have had being alone in the world. They gave each other friendship. As theologian Eugene Rogers once said at the wedding of friends: "In the friendship of the best sort, says Aristotle, the friends make each other better. As Naomi became to Ruth a teacher, and Ruth became to Naomi more than seven sons . . . In faith we grant time to desire's risk and friendship's work."

Embracing the Gift of Naomi and Ruth

Plan to spend some time alone with your mother or your daughter, or with the person who is *like* your mother or your daughter. Call it a "Mother and Daughter Day." Just the two of you together. It could be a weekend journey you go off on, or, if you don't have a "hanging out together" relationship, it could be a walk down the road or going out for lunch. Even if your relationship is at times (or always!) strained and complicated (whose isn't?), on some level, you probably have a deep loyalty to each other that ultimately ends up putting the hassles of trying to get along in perspective.

The ritual of Naomi and Ruth has two parts: it honors your loyalty, which is grounded in the years of your connectedness, and it bids you to inquire. You may ask, Who is the person before me now? Am I relating to the person who is here before me now, or are we both in a time warp? The agenda of your "Mother and Daughter Day" is to pay attention to who each of you is right now and to try to encounter each other in fresh ways. Imagine you are meeting for the first time as strangers, temporarily freed of all your history together and all the old patterns and expectations.

I would be the first to acknowledge how unlikely it would be for me to go off with my mother and say, "What habitual ways do we have of relating to each other, based on who we were once and are no longer?" My mother would either say, "I need this like I need a hole in my head," or complain that wherever we were, it was too chilly and we'd get sick with pneumonia, or too hot and we'd pass out, or too smoky and we'd die from secondhand smoke. For us, the phone works better, as we each feel safe, comfortable, and in control speaking from our own turf.

If a calm, face-to-face, analytical discussion about relationships is not something you can pull off with your mother and if even the phone feels like a stretch, it might be possible with your daughters. (I'm not the only one who has observed that intergenerational relationships are much less fraught with tension these days. Reports are saying that college students e-mail or call home daily because they really want to hear their parents' advice.)

Recently, I went off with one of my daughters on a long ride into the Virginia countryside and, in the spirit of Naomi and Ruth, I told her something about our relationship that had been on my mind. "When you make decisions that concern me," I said, "I can tell you're trying to guess what I want. You're generous to take my feelings into consideration, and maybe there was a time when that worked for us because I had a hard time expressing what I really wanted. But I can do that now. Just ask me what I want. No need to psych me out. I don't want you to decide not to spend the weekend away with friends because you think I'll be lonely if I'm home by myself with you and Dad away. *Ask* me if I'll be lonely. Let *me* be the one to tell you whether I'll be perfectly fine all alone." She understood just what I meant, and we were *both* able to break old habits.

PART IV

BEING A PARENT

CHAPTER 10

SARAH
PROTECTING
YOUR DREAMS

The Biblical Story

Sarai was barren, she had no child. . . . Sarai, Abram's wife, had not given him children. She had an Egyptian maid named Hagar. Sarai said to Abram, "As you can see, the Lord has kept me from bearing. Have relations with my maid and perhaps I shall have a son through her." Abram did as she asked. . . . Hagar bore Abram a son, and Abram named the son Ishmael.

When Abram was ninety-nine years old . . . God said to him, "Your name will be Abraham. . . . As for your wife, Sarai, you shall not call her Sarai, but Sarah. I will bless her; indeed, I will give you a son by her. I will bless her and she shall give rise to nations; kings of people shall come from her."

Abraham fell on his face and laughed. In his heart, he said to himself, "Can a child be born to a man a hundred years old, or can Sarah give birth at ninety?"

God said, "Nevertheless, Sarah, your wife, shall bear you a son, and you shall call him Isaac. I will keep my covenant with him as an everlasting covenant for his offspring. . . . I will keep my covenant with Isaac, whom Sarah shall bear to you at this season next year."

The Lord appeared to Abraham by the oaks of Mamre. He was sitting at the entrance of his tent as the day grew hot. Lifting his eyes, he saw three men standing over him. When he saw them, he ran from the entrance of the tent to greet them and, bowing to the earth, said, "My lords, if it please you, do not go on past your servant. Let a little water be brought; wash your feet and recline under the tree. Let me fetch a bit of bread so that you may refresh yourselves; then continue on your way. . . . "

Abraham hastened into the tent to Sarah and said, "Quick, three measures of choice flour! Knead it and make cakes!" . . . He took curds and milk and the calf that had been prepared and set these before them; and he waited on them under the tree as they ate.

They said to him, "Where is your wife, Sarah?"

He replied, "There, in the tent."

One said, "I will return to you next year, and your wife, Sarah, shall have a son!"

Sarah was listening at the entrance of the tent, which was behind him. Now Abraham and Sarah were old, advanced in years; Sarah no longer menstruated. Sarah laughed to herself, saying, "Now that I am withered, is there to be pleasure for me? My husband is so old!"

Then the Lord said to Abraham, "Why did Sarah laugh and say, 'Shall I really bear a child, now that I am old?' Is anything too wondrous for the Lord? I will return to you at this time next year, and Sarah shall have a son."

Sarah pretended, saying, "I did not laugh," for she was afraid.

But God replied, "No, you did laugh."

God took note of Sarah as promised. . . . Sarah became pregnant and bore a son to Abraham in his old age, at the time of which God had spoken. Abraham named his newborn son, whom Sarah had borne him, Isaac. . . . Sarah said, "God has made laughter for me; everyone who hears will laugh for me." And she added,

"Who would have said to Abraham that Sarah would nurse children? Well, I have borne a son in his old age."

—Adapted from Genesis 11:30; 16:1–2, 15; 17:15–19, 21;
18:1–15; 21:1–7

Sarah's Own Story

The horizon was still. Their horses, which would tremble when they detected even small shifts in distant sands, were calm. Yet, in the brightening morning light, Sarah anticipated there would be guests today who would require endless fussing. Were she certain, she'd have ground extra wheat or eyed the flocks to decide which calf was the fattest of the lot. With only a suspicion, she conserved energy by tidying her tent more deliberately and by noting the provisions she had on hand. She was a woman in her eighties—whether or not she remembered to preserve her strength, her body did so automatically, moving along at a slower pace, obliging her to stop and sigh.

If having visitors required no more than offering shade and water, Sarah would have found that small imposition worthwhile. She enjoyed being diverted by news and company. But no visitor could be received without fanfare. However much Sarah once relished company, these days it was just too much. Today was no different. But as she lost herself in tidying the tent, she began to feel curious about what the day might bring.

The results of her hasty stocktaking were promising. Sarah had dried figs, olives, hard goat cheese, and lemons preserved in salt on hand. If she baked bread, she could quickly fix a suitable meal. The remaining problem, the same problem she had lived with for years, was Abraham's overwhelming anxiety about receiving visitors. How many times he and Sarah had successfully entertained guests lavishly and precisely according to their customs—with foot washings, ceremonial hand washings, cups of blessing, formal toasts, attention to the guests' safe departure. Still, Abraham never stopped worrying about performing the protocol correctly and doing well by their guests. The work of preparing the food had never been a burden for Sarah. It was calming to Abraham, reassuring him beforehand that she had cooked and chopped enough, keeping him busy in his own tasks so he didn't start monitoring her and meddling. It got no better when the guests departed. Abraham reviewed the visit in detail, and he inevitably saw only their shortcomings. He had not washed their feet with enough gentleness or found a shady place for their animals; Sarah had not sweetened the tea to their liking. Small things, which he spun out of proportion.

What had prompted Abraham's relentless critique? Sarah imagined that Abraham believed God was punishing them with childlessness for some offense they had done to a passing guest. It was not a rational explanation, she knew. But she understood that Abraham needed something on which to pin this misfortune that followed them like a shadow. No other explanation—that God had forgotten them, that they had misunderstood God's promise—would have been tolerable.

Sarah used to try teasing Abraham about his anxieties, so out of proportion as they were, for the hospitality of Sarah and Abraham was legendary. But you couldn't tease Abraham. "You have no sense of humor," she'd tell him, and that made him smile a little, because he knew she was correct. But there was no changing his disposition. He was all seriousness, getting no jokes, no puns. He saw horseplay among the young men who traveled with them as a waste of time and energy. He was a loving man, and warm too, but as he saw it, play was for children and so was laughter.

On this morning, Sarah recognized that she, too, had laughed little in her days. But she knew she could laugh. She was waiting for the right opportunity. A child in her belly would make her laugh. If lovemaking could lead to a little person who would emerge months later and say, "Here I am! I'm yours!" she would laugh.

The morning turned into a full day and still there were no certain signs of visitors. Sarah felt a continuous, sustained agitation in the air, a sense that something was on the verge of happening and that their lives would change in ways that would surprise, even transform them. With each hour, Sarah became more convinced of the imminent arrival, not just of guests but also of laughter that would enter their lives.

She was about to stick her head outside her tent and blurt out her premonition to Abraham, so that at least he could prepare, even if in some preliminary way. But she held her tongue. Why put him through the anguish of anticipating guests if it were for naught? Sarah sat back on her heels—which she could still do at her age, and not topple over, much to her pride. She reached under her bedding for a small box.

Sarah never told this to a soul, but from the time she was fifteen she had been putting away tiny treasures that she would pass on to a child of her own, and she continued to add to it throughout her life. She now took these treasures out of the carved olive-wood box that held them. Here was the first earring that had been threaded in her ear as an infant. Here was a sliver of a clay idol belonging to Abraham's father, Terach, so the child would know of forebears, of paths not taken, of the whole story. Here was a rock of many glittering facets that she had discovered on the ground on her wedding day. She had taken the rock as a sign that she lived in a world in which promises were kept.

When she was newly married and failed to conceive, older mothers told Sarah she was better off without children. With children, they'd say, you are vulnerable; with children, your heart will break each time they are hurt, each time they leave your sight. As she grew old and remained childless, it was the younger mothers, their hair always limp, always drained by the demands of too many babies, who told Sarah the very same thing, thinking they could console her. No words provided comfort, not now, not years earlier. Sarah had been too certain about what she had wanted, what she had dreamed for. The dream, however late in coming, still seemed possible then. She would have her child, and how she would laugh.

When her periods stopped coming, she knew the dream was never to be.

Then on this day, without a single sound of voices, without any sound of weary animals panting for water, three guests arrived at the door of Abraham's tent as if they had come from a dream. "Peace be upon you, Father Abraham, and to Mother Sarah," they said, in voices so soft and muffled you couldn't tell if they were old or young, men or women. Sarah suspected they were not regular travelers. They were wrapped in desert garb, but they had no baggage, not even empty skins for water, and there were no animals with them. Might they be angels of God who would shake up their lives with the joys and sorrows that only parents know?

Sarah could see that the visitors, like three small dunes of golden sand, had seated themselves in the shade of an oak tree and drank from the cups of water that Abraham had thrust into their hands. From the shadows on Abraham's tent, Sarah observed his frenzied movement. She heard the nervous cracking in his voice as he repeated, "Blessed be those who have come from afar."

Abraham raced into Sarah's tent. She knew he would soon be dispatching her to make cakes. Abraham caught his breath. Sarah watched as he stilled his body, as if planting it into the earth. He whispered, "These are not regular visitors. I'm telling you, Sarah . . ." He started again, "Sarah, I am saying . . ." He slapped his thigh with his right hand. He slapped his chest with both hands. He strutted about before Sarah, cocking his head, mimicking the way he once had tried to gain her attention before they were betrothed.

Laughing, Sarah fell back onto her heels, nearly toppling over. Abraham extended his hands to her and they clasped wrists. He lifted her to her feet, and as she rose, she embraced him strongly and held him still. She parted her clothes and his. Sarah laughed again to think that her body might still remember how to make love. Holding Abraham close, she felt the laughter in all of his flesh.

Sarah Speaks to Us

You'll never know what it's like to want a child your whole life, and then, like Sarah, discover you are expecting at the age of ninety. But you may know what it's like to spend many years wanting something very much, so much that the desire defines you or depletes you. It could be the dream of having a child; it could be a goal that had to be put on hold, or one that remained outside your reach.

Like Sarah, you may have had the experience of belatedly getting what you've yearned for and not knowing quite how to react. Had your dream come true when you had hoped it would, you might have felt grateful that your life was swimming along its course as you had imagined it should. If the dream took just a bit longer than you expected, or if it required more hard work than you had imagined, you might have been ecstatic when it came true. The cosmos was finally smiling down on you, rewarding you for your tenacity, determination, and patience.

Dreams that come belatedly true can be disconcerting. You're a different person now. You have different desires, different definitions of happiness and fulfillment. You may have resigned yourself to healing from the disappointment. You may have changed the course of your life altogether.

You don't mean to be ungrateful, but the truth is, the fulfillment of the dream doesn't mean the same thing anymore. If at forty-two you finally get pregnant, or at forty-seven you finally get a job in the field you've trained in, or at fifty-three you finally meet your life partner, you're happy, but you may not be dancing the same jig you would have danced years before. Others may not understand your muddled feelings. You don't want to present yourself as hardened or embittered, so you keep your complicated feelings to yourself.

While the old saying in Proverbs "Hope deferred sickens the heart. But desire realized is a tree of life" (Proverbs 13:12) seems true, it obscures part of the story. The pain of a hope deferred for too long leaves its mark on you, and even if your desire is eventually realized, you can still feel wounded. As Langston Hughes once wrote, a dream deferred can either feel like an explosion, or like "a raisin in the sun."

Sarah models how we can respond to dreams that become belatedly fulfilled. We can laugh. And what a complicated, bittersweet laugh it is, reminding us that it's very human to feel joy and sorrow at the same time.

The biblical Sarai had accompanied Abram on a spiritual journey to the land of Canaan. This was a journey that transformed them both, as indicated by God's giving them new names—Sarah and Abraham—suggesting that their lives had been touched and changed by the presence of God. Sarah left home, just as Abraham did, with the expectation that if they had the courage to follow God's way and if they kept their pact with God, staying in an obedient, loving relationship, they would be showered with blessings. If Abraham was most enthused by the possibility of becoming the father of a great nation, the blessing that mattered most to Sarah was more tangible and of the here-and-now—it was having a child who would maintain the same partnership with God that she and Abraham were cultivating. Knowing she would have a child to love and fill with a dramatically new vision of how to be human gave her identity, meaning, and focus. It could keep her going through days of hot, dry sand.

Meeting God, and pleasing God, Abraham and Sarah had always felt blessed. But the sign that would confirm that feeling and make it tangible would be a child.

Sarah spent a lifetime anticipating this child that never came. But Sarah never became pregnant, however long she and Abraham tried and waited. She wanted the baby for herself, and as the text makes clear, she wanted the baby for Abraham's sake, as a sign that this God whom they had chosen to follow kept promises. Dejected, but still able to act pragmatically, Sarah encouraged Abraham to have a child with her Egyptian servant, Hagar. If Sarah couldn't have her own biological child, at least she could find a way to help Abraham feel affirmed by God. Might Hagar's child, who would symbolically count as her own, help her feel affirmed by God? Sarah didn't know, but how could she not take the chance?

Meanwhile, Sarah discovered other opportunities to be maternal and matriarchal. She got on with her life, finding alternative ways to express herself, to give love and find fulfillment. The ancient legends (which cannot bear to think of Sarah the Matriarch languishing or being despondent) say she became a teacher and spiritual guide, teaching women about God and God's covenant. She was a hostess extraordinaire, whose capacious tent was a place where travelers on their own journeys could feel temporarily at home and could become refreshed and emboldened enough to continue on their own paths. The legends of the Midrash insist that Sarah was graced with an abundant spiritual presence; a cloud of divine presence was with her always: "As long as Sarah lived, there was a blessing on her dough, and the lamp used to burn from the evening of the Sabbath until the evening of the following Sabbath; when she died, these ceased." She never cut off her conversation with God; she prayed continually for a child of her own, even beyond the point of biological possibility. God took pleasure in hearing her voice. Indirectly, through Abraham, God continued to bolster hope, even when Sarah was so old and surely well beyond hoping anymore: "I will bless Sarah; I will give you a son by her." If you hold a picture of a pregnant Grandma Moses in your mind's eye, you can't help but wonder if Sarah found God's reiterated promise—which one imagines Abraham, in good faith, relayed—more cruel and mocking than reassuring.

Though the story of Sarah's laughter in the face of God's prediction that a son would come to her in old age is the better known one, in fact, it was Abraham who, quite literally, had the first laugh. He responded viscerally and authentically to God's promise (relayed through the visiting angels) of a child in old age by throwing himself on his face, laughing, and saying to himself, "Can a child be born to a man of a hundred years old, or can Sarah bear a child at ninety?" "Yes," said God, "it will happen this time next year"—and not only that—"you shall name him Isaac and I will keep my covenant with him and his offspring."

Abraham's laughter was passed over with neither remark nor consequence. His laughter, the commentators understood, was but an innocent mark of his astonishment and not a sign of diminished trust in God's promise or capacity to work wonders. (How did the commentators know this? Using a curious form of logic—the implausibility factor—relied on frequently enough: How do we know Abraham didn't doubt God? Because it was unthinkable that a man like Abraham could have a doubting bone in his body!)

Soon after, three men—indeed, they were angels—appeared at Abraham's tent. He extended every hospitality toward them and then raced to Sarah's tent to enlist her help in making fancy cakes. After feasting, the angels asked Abraham where his wife was, and he pointed to her in her own tent. One angel reiterated God's promise, or perhaps it was God in the guise of an angel, for he spoke in the first person, saying: "I will return to you next year, and you will have a son."

Sarah had been listening from her tent, not because she was eavesdropping, but because the practice then (as it still is in some devout Muslim families) was for men and women to dine separately in the presence of company. Women who wanted to hear news of the outside world and still respect their culture's rules of gender separation had to keep their ears open.

Hearing the angel's oath, Sarah reflected on the irony and the impossibility of it all. Abraham was old. She was not only old as well, she had stopped menstruating long ago! So Sarah laughed to herself, just as Abraham had. For her, too, it was a spontaneous reaction, but unlike Abraham, who laughed while in conversation with God, Sarah believed she was emoting in privacy. She herself did not fully understand the meaning of her complicated laughter and went on to clarify her feelings for herself. "Now that I am worn, is there to be pleasure for me? My husband is so old!" It is not clear how Sarah meant "pleasure." She may have been referring to the pleasure of continuing to have sexual relations with Abraham, or she may have meant that she struggled to imagine how a woman the age of a grandmother could still have the pleasure of giving birth to a baby and raising it.

When Sarah laughed, God responded with anger. How dare Sarah doubt the words of the prophetic angel! After all, was anything too hard for God? God was angrier still when Sarah denied her laughter. Yet God did not take the issue up directly with Sarah. God went to Abraham and asked: "Why did Sarah laugh?" It was not a question, an expression of curiosity. It was an accusation, which the commentators used to suggest that Sarah's laughter was distinct from Abraham's. Hers was a sign of disbelief, mistrust, lack of faith in God, who had the power to do anything, including allowing a very old woman to give birth.

At this point, God misquoted Sarah to Abraham, so as not (according to legend) to bring about marital discord. To spare Abraham from hearing that Sarah couldn't imagine having a child with someone as old as he, and to keep the peace in their household, God reported that Sarah said it was *her* age alone that made birth at this late day incredulous: "Shall I in truth bear a child, old as I am?" God repeated the promise, coupled with some rebuke: "Is anything too wondrous for the Lord? I will return to you at this time next year, and Sarah shall have a son."

Although God was not speaking directly to Sarah, she spoke to God, frustrated that her laughter was misread as disbelief and not for the astonishment it was. "Sarah lied saying, 'I did not laugh,' for she was frightened." I think she was saying that while she may have in fact laughed, God had misread its meaning.

But God did not grasp the clarification that Sarah tried to offer, and replied, "You did laugh."

God's promise was remembered. Sarah gave birth to Isaac, whose name not only means "laughter," but in Hebrew, *Yitzchak*, actually sounds like a little guffaw. At his circumcision ceremony, Sarah said with relief and thanksgiving, "God has brought me laughter; everyone who hears will laugh with me." Though she had been chided once for the way she expressed her astonishment, she continued to speak from her heart: "Who would have said to Abraham that Sarah would suckle children, yet I have borne a child in his old age." (Genesis 21:7)

Allegra Goodman's short story "Sarah" tells a modern version of the story of Sarah and the dreams that she has held on to, which brings the tale home to us. Goodman's Sarah is a fifty-six-year-old woman, a mother of four grown children, and a writer who is teaching an adult education class in "Creative Midrash," combining creative writing and Bible study. In the rush of family life and in supporting her husband's career, Sarah's own writing never really took off. True, while she once had a novel published by a small press and now writes book reviews for periodicals, she mostly shares her poetry with an audience of her friends and family. She has accomplishments she can be proud of, but she would be the first to admit she had not become the Shakespeare or Donne of her generation.

Her students ask her if she has ever been inspired by the Bible to write her own story. Years ago, she had indeed written about the biblical Sarah and her reflections on being a mother. But when Sarah thinks of the verses about biblical Sarah now, she sees them afresh. Unlike the biblical Sarah who pined for children, Goodman's Sarah had children easily enough. What *she* pined for was to have literary success, to be discovered. Whereas the biblical Sarah laughed when God told her that at her advanced age she would give birth to a child, Goodman's Sarah knows she would surely laugh if an angel of God—or better yet, a literary agent from New York—came to her and said, "'You, Sarah, will write a great novel, a best seller . . . ,' then she would laugh for all to hear—although she would take down the phone number of the agent just in case."[1] Not that Sarah wouldn't welcome success and find it satisfying on some level, but it no longer defined her happiness. She would laugh because other accomplishments had come to define happiness and success in the meantime, for example, her ability to peaceably resolve family crises.

Maybe you know what it feels like to have a dream that has been deferred for so long that you can hardly remember how intense your desire once was or how painful the disappointment was each time you got close to achieving what you hoped for. Maybe it felt like it just wasn't meant to be, and you tentatively gave up. Other dreams and goals crept in, and some of those, you did achieve, and your life moved along and got whole again. Until something happened to bring back the longing and made you think, if only. If only I had finished graduate school. If only I had been chosen in one of the auditions. If only we had had a child before the divorce. If only I had tried living in a big city or open-ing a café. If only I hadn't let other people's needs and dreams take pri-ority over my own. If only I had had better luck, or had known someone who could have opened a door for me. If only.

Sarah's laughter gives us perspective on our yearning. We can hear her laughter when we hold on to our dreams and when we decide it's time to relinquish them.

Sarah encourages us, on one hand, to stay tenacious, even when a reasonable person would have long ago given up, even when others tease us about our dogged pursuit, and even when others feel our pursuit of a goal inconveniences them. Sarah tells those who are seeking to have babies through technological means that were once unthinkable that the effort, anguish, and expense can result in a miracle baby (or two, or three . . .). She tells us to go back to school at age fifty, to learn to fly, to join the Peace Corps.

On the other hand, Sarah also encourages us to revise our long-held goals in the same ways we are free to update a résumé or renovate a kitchen. She supports us when we acknowledge that the things we once thought might give us ultimate happiness or define our lives turn out not to have the meaning we once thought they would.

With the aid of Sarah's wisdom, I have gained perspective on some of my own yearnings. Sarah has helped me better understand how my definitions of happiness have changed over the years. I spent most of my twenties obsessively yearning to discover if I really had the talent to be a writer, and I would look frantically for signs of approval. I was ready to work hard at my craft, but if I didn't have the talent, I wanted to know it. My dream then was to have someone in the writing world (i.e., not my husband, parents, or friends who all seemed too free with their praise) say, "You're the real thing!" as if it were the Good Housekeep-ing Seal of Approval. I had two small children at home then. I was the only one in my circle of girlfriends who had married and started a fam-ily. While they were climbing up their respective professional ladders, I was struggling to find the time and energy to write between naptime, diaper time, and bedtime. Comparing myself to my friends who effi-ciently went on to earn advanced degrees, get full-time jobs, and sup-port themselves on real, grown-up salaries, I felt like I had failed to live up to my promise.

Running in from my mailbox with the self-addressed envelopes containing manuscripts that had bounced back to me, I scrutinized my manuscripts like a forensics expert for any indication of a smidgen of an editor's approval. Eventually, I started getting handwritten letters of overt encouragement. You'd think the encouraging words would have satisfied my yearnings and placated the self-doubt, but now I saw publication as the new sign of my being good enough. Publication of stories and essays in small journals followed, and you'd think that would have surely done the trick. It didn't (except for a few moments of elation and jumping around). I had graduated to higher expectations. It's not that I didn't celebrate the accomplishment of my earliest publications—at least I felt I could now honestly say that I was a "real" writer, and not just an aspiring one—but I wanted to be taken seriously. If only I could get my work published in places people had actually heard of. By the time I started publishing in the *New York Times* and glossy magazines, I was finally convinced that I had talent, and I was feeling respected by others.

You'd think I would have been happy at last. That's what I thought would happen. But now I had newer, higher aspirations. I'm not alone in this feeling. My colleague at the University of Virginia, psychologist Tim Wilson, who studies why it's hard for people to anticipate what will actually make them happy, explains the phenomenon this way in a September 2003 article by Jon Gertner, in the *New York Times Magazine*: "We don't realize how quickly we will adapt to a pleasurable event and make it the backdrop of our lives. When any event occurs to us, we make it ordinary. And through becoming ordinary, we lose our pleasure."[2]

As many of us have done, I exasperated even myself by the escalation of my desires, laughing at myself, but it was a sad laugh. Was I ever going to be able to tell myself I did a good job without feeling that if I stopped there and didn't advance to the next level of accomplishment, I was a nobody? Would no accomplishment ever convince me I was good enough?

I told myself that having a book published would make me happy-ever-after. Then my first book got published, and soon I was yearning to publish a second book to demonstrate that I had more than one book in me. After my second book, I kept on wanting. Now I wanted to be self-supporting as a writer, which is possible but really hard. I was anxious to do it, to assure myself that if anything ever happened to my husband, I could support my girls and myself. We moved to a bigger city for easier contact with my editors, and I took any assignment that came my way. My wake-up moment came when I was writing one lightweight piece on cranberries and another on pool toys. Cranberries? Pool toys? What was I doing writing about things that didn't matter to me? Engrossed in making a successful career, I had lost the joy and dignity of writing well about things I cared about. What had begun as a passion became a job.

It didn't happen overnight, but somewhere along the way I stopped defining happiness or measuring myself by my writing. I took an academic position that allowed me to earn my living teaching, and that gave me the freedom to write only about things that mattered to me.

This past August, I went hiking in the Blue Ridge Mountains with my family. Bringing up the rear of our little entourage, I laughed to myself. "This is what happiness looks like. This is what accomplishment looks like—to have raised this always-interesting family. I have this late summer day, these delicious and complicated people I love so dearly, the cool waterfalls up ahead, the thought of stopping soon to have peanut butter and jelly sandwiches. There's nothing more I need or want."

Tripping on a mossy boulder, I sensed the presence of Sarah deeply. She reminded me, "Stop measuring your happiness. It's all distinctly precious."

Embracing the Gift of Sarah

When people pray for God's help, they often evoke the patriarchs and matriarchs and request their intercession. "Blessed are you, God of Abraham, Isaac, Jacob, Sarah, Rebecca, Rachel, and Leah." The hope is that if only for the merit of their ancestors, God will pay attention to their call. They may also hope the ancient ancestors will alert God: "One of my kinfolk needs help!" Legends hold that our mother Sarah, in particular, has a strong ability to protect her descendants and keep them out of harm's way.

In that spirit, we can invoke Sarah to protect our dreams, lighting a candle to ask for her attention. We can ask her to help us pursue our dreams wisely, with the appropriate doggedness, and to know when they might be better laid to rest for a while, or even forever. We ask her to assure us that if we choose to relinquish a dream, it is not a betrayal. We ask her to help us notice when the closing of one door signals the opening of another. She can give us the strength to laugh when our good dreams come true at inappropriate or just curious times. While Sarah joins us in appreciating the irony of a dream belatedly fulfilled, we ask her to keep us from being too cynical or bitter to accept good tidings that come our way and celebrate them for what they can mean to us now, even when they come clumsily out of season.

Sarah will keep us from saying, "Too little, too late," and will help us say instead, "Better late than never."

You might offer this blessing: May I be blessed, as our mother Sarah was, to receive dreams that come true in their own season.

CHAPTER 11

REBECCA
RAISING A FAMILY
IN PARTNERSHIP

The Biblical Story

Lifting up her eyes, Rebecca saw Isaac. She got down from her camel and asked his servant, "Who is that man walking in the field toward us?" The servant said, "That is my master." She took a veil and covered herself. . . . Isaac brought her into the tent of his mother, Sarah, and he took Rebecca as his wife. Isaac loved her, and thus was comforted after his mother's death. . . .

Isaac was forty years old when he took Rebecca as his wife. . . . Isaac pleaded with the Lord on behalf of his wife because she was barren, and the Lord responded to his plea, and his wife, Rebecca, became pregnant. But the children struggled in her womb and she said, "If this is so, why do I exist?" She went to inquire of the Lord and the Lord answered her, "Two nations are in your womb, two people apart while still in your body. One people shall be mightier than the other, and the older shall serve the younger." When her time to give birth was at hand, there were twins in her womb. . . . When the boys grew up, Esau became a skillful hunter, a man of the outdoors; but Jacob was a mild man who stayed among the tents. Isaac favored Esau because he hunted game, but Rebecca loved Jacob.

[Rebecca urges Jacob to impersonate Esau so that he might receive his father's blessing. Technically the blessing belongs to Esau, but it is God's wish for it to go to Jacob. Jacob hesitates to go along with his mother's plan.]

"If my father touches me, he shall know I am a trickster, and I will be cursed and not blessed." But Rebecca answered him, "Your curse will be upon me. Just do as I say," and he did so.

Rebecca said to Isaac, "I am disgusted with my life because of the native women. If Jacob marries a Hittite woman like these . . . what good will life be to me?" So Isaac sent for Jacob and blessed him. He instructed him, "You shall not take a wife among the Canaanite women." And Jacob listened to his father and mother.

Esau held a grudge against Jacob because of the blessing that his father had given him, and Esau said to himself, "After I have mourned for my father, I will kill my brother Jacob." . . . When these words were reported to Rebecca, she sent for Jacob and said . . . "Flee at once to Haran. . . . Let me not lose the both of my sons in one day."

—Adapted from Genesis 24–28

Rebecca's Own Story

Rebecca can feel it, and perhaps Isaac knows it, too—these are among Isaac's last days, and lying beside each other in the dark as they try to fall asleep, they summon back images and snippets of conversation from their past. Between the two of them, one memory sparking another, they piece together a family story.

"They had you picked out for me: the perfect girl from my parents' clan back in Canaan. Lovely, strong, and hospitable," said Isaac.

"I was very young, but I knew my mind," said Rebecca.

"That hasn't changed, " said Isaac.

"I could have waited, you know, till I was older, but I agreed to travel to meet you immediately. Your people draped me in silver and gold jewels and tucked beaded ornaments in my hair. I took one look at you and fell off my camel."

"That's when I fell in love with you," Isaac replied. "When we married, you brought me out of my darkness after my mother Sarah's death. But then you knew your own darkness. How you yearned for children, how we waited and nothing happened. Was it twenty years?"

"Remember how you prayed to God for me? I was too upset to pray."

"I prayed to God for both of us, and you got pregnant."

"I wanted a child with all my life," Rebecca said. "Do you remember how much I hated being pregnant?"

"Of course I remember. Finally you become pregnant, and you want to die. I didn't know what to do—I was ready to bury you."

"I said I *thought* I would die. What did I say then?" Rebecca asked.

"You said, 'If this is so, why do I exist?' "

"I said that? Why would I have said that?"

"Because you couldn't go on. There was nothing I could say or do. You said you would go yourself to talk to God. You wouldn't let me speak for you."

"I did talk to God," Rebecca said. "God told me I would have twins and that the older child would rule over the younger."

"So you maintained," said Isaac.

"You didn't believe me," Rebecca said. "I believed you when you spoke to God. Why didn't you believe that God had told me how the future would unfold?"

"I was already sixty when the babies were born," said Isaac. "I didn't believe I would become a father. That was enough of a miracle. Twins, not twins, one ruling over the other—it's not that I didn't believe you—it didn't matter to me."

"You should have known it mattered to me. I didn't know if it was a curse or a promise. So I tried to forget. But when we saw the boys were so different from the start, we knew to brace ourselves. I saw you watching Esau going off into the fields with his bow and arrow. That made you so happy, to have this son who was aggressive and could take care of himself. You lived through him."

"I took pleasure in Esau; you can't take that away from me," said Isaac. "And you preferred when Jacob stayed around the home to cook porridge with you. I never understood that. I didn't understand Jacob, but I accepted he was different. I would have blessed him for being himself—he didn't have to pretend to be just like Esau."

"I didn't care for those girls, Esau's first wives, Judith and Basemat," said Rebecca, changing the subject.

"They could have kept you company, like daughters."

"If you had seen how they acted toward me, you wouldn't have cared for them either. But you went blind. Shall I tell you why God gave you the gift of blindness?" Rebecca asked.

"A gift?"

"So you wouldn't have to see what you didn't want to see," she said.

"You took advantage of me, Rebecca, making Jacob disguise himself as Esau, to steal Esau's blessing. I told you then and I am still telling you, you both took advantage."

"Don't blame Jacob. He didn't want to deceive you. I told him he had to. The blame should be on me."

"You think I blessed Jacob because you had both tricked me?" Isaac asked. "Maybe that's what I had already decided to do. Maybe I tricked you both. Do you remember how furious Esau was when he found out? But he never blamed me."

"Not you, but he was ready to kill Jacob," Rebecca said. "You couldn't see the anger in his face. I had to be the one to tell Jacob, 'Flee for your life!'"

"With all that going on, you were still carrying on about Jacob marrying a local girl and not someone from your family back home. Do you remember what you said then?" Isaac asked. "You said, 'I am disgusted with my life.' Your whole life? That hurt me."

"I was talking about then, that moment. It wasn't about you. Jacob had a responsibility, a line to carry on. I had to make that happen. Remember how you sat Jacob down before he left? You said to me, 'Let me talk to the boy. He'll listen to me.' You made him promise to listen to his mother and marry the right girl; otherwise he would lose the power of his blessing. He listened to you. He did the right thing. You never told me what you said to him. That this was the only way he would be blessed?"

"He didn't understand what it meant to carry the weight of a blessing. So I told him, 'Do what your mother says or she will be impossible for me to live with.' That he understood."

"Still, he listened to you. He went off to Haran and he married girls from the family. Jacob, he was a good boy. They were both good boys. We raised good boys together."

Rebecca Speaks to Us

No single episode in the lives of Rebecca and Isaac demonstrates that either has great aptitude as a parent. Individual snapshots would show one messy drama after another: Rebecca hysterical about her pregnancy; both parents playing favorites with their twin sons; Rebecca taking easy advantage of Isaac when he is old and blind, tricking him into blessing her favorite son, Jacob, the son she deemed to be the more worthy one to inherit the patriarchal mantle.

But if we look at their lives in a more cumulative fashion, we see that Rebecca and Isaac knew how necessary it was to collaborate in raising a family. When life posed challenges, Rebecca and Isaac improvised ways to respond. Theirs was a long dance of give and take between loving and complicated people. Their partnership worked. They drew upon each other's strengths as they muddled through life. They allowed each other to grow and change, both as a married couple and as parents.

Looking at the big picture, for that is what Rebecca is asking us to do in our own child-rearing partnerships, you'll see that while there was the inevitable friction, there was also plenty of grace and understanding between them, too.

Couples raising children are awarded no prizes for coexisting effectively, making mistakes, giving and getting second chances, forgiving and forgetting, and being supported and being supportive over the years. Maybe they should be.

Rebecca and Isaac's give-and-take style provides insights as we try to work out cooperative models in our own parenting. Their insights are clearly relevant for traditional, two-parent families. But they are true just as well for families of all kinds of complicated blendings, in which various combinations of adults—steps and exes, beloved partners and hands-on aunts, uncles, and godparents—work together over time and, despite the messiness of it all, choreograph ways to share the task of bringing up kids.

Before we encounter Rebecca and Isaac as part of a partnership, we need to meet each one individually to see what each brings to the relationship.

Rebecca is the most fully drawn of all the matriarchs. At the outset, she was a luscious young woman of marriageable age, a good catch from a good family. In the idyllic pastoral setting, she stood by a spring, drawing water for the servant of Abraham, who had come seeking a wife for young Isaac. She was outgoing and acted with generosity, drawing water by herself for both the servant and his camels and inviting him to spend the night. Her endearing traits were quickly apparent to the servant. With the marriage arrangements in motion, she was bedecked with the jewels she had received as tokens from the family of her intended: a nose ring (a less punkish gesture in those days) and golden bracelets on her arms. We know she had free will in this matter, for she was not given, without her consent, to be Isaac's bride. She had gumption, the willingness to leave her family and travel to Canaan. She was a woman of some means, with a dowry of handmaidens and camels to accompany her into married life. She knew how to ride a camel, although one legend suggests she was so smitten and dazzled when she saw Isaac for the first time that she fell off!

Once married, Rebecca was deeply loved by her husband and experienced God's presence and blessing in her union. Like other matriarchs, she was barren initially. She lived with disappointment, self-doubt, and yearning. When the children she did have grew up, she engineered a plan for her younger son, Jacob—the one she knew had more leadership potential—to disguise himself in goatskins so as to receive the blessing that should have rightfully gone to his older brother Esau. We know Rebecca was persuasive too, for while Jacob initially hesitated to go along with her plan, he was won over when she promised she would bear any curse that came about as a consequence of the ruse. We gather that Rebecca acted as she did because she felt responsible to see that Jacob take on the patriarchal mantle, in accordance with God's plan.

What do we know about Isaac? He was a beloved, belated child, adored by both his elderly parents, Abraham and Sarah. He may have been doted on, and this may have spoiled him, but it's possible that the surfeit of love may have given him a deep sense of his worth. As a young man, he was nearly sacrificed as a sign of his father's divine devotion. After the near-sacrifice, we never hear from Isaac's mother, Sarah, again until her death scene, leading one to speculate that she was killed by her powerlessness to stop Abraham and the agony she experienced as her son was led off, presumably, to die in the name of her husband's god. We can only surmise that such a traumatic experience made its mark on Isaac. Was he a person of great resilience who emerged convinced that even life's bleakest scenarios can have happy resolutions? Or was he left permanently wounded, saddled with fears of abandonment and a tendency to mistrust? The way Isaac moved on with his life and formed relationships with his wife and sons suggests he had the ability to bounce back.

Even before Rebecca and Isaac had children, they were developing a cooperative style of being together. Consider how Isaac responded to Rebecca when, after twenty years of being infertile (recall that in those days, infertility was assumed to be a female problem) she lost hope that she would ever conceive. Isaac deeply empathized with Rebecca. He didn't have to ask her how she felt and she didn't need to tell him: he knew, and this spurred him to action. He pleaded to God on Rebecca's behalf, arguing robustly and successfully. Rebecca trusted Isaac to carry her sorrow before God, not only because she knew her husband empathized with her sorrow but also because he shared her dreams. She trusted in the competence of his prayers.

In addition, a division of parenting labor is going on here, based on talents. Isaac is good at making requests of God; as an old man, we see he is skilled in discerning which blessing his children will need in life (even if he can't quite tell who is who!). Rebecca, we learn, is better at approaching God to anticipate what her children's futures will be. Rebecca is better at making things happen, pushing them along. Isaac is better at accepting what is before him.

In my own marriage, my husband and I have become increasingly aware of our individual strengths and weaknesses in parenting—we've been at it for twenty-five years now. Sometimes we can be interchangeable. Our daughters will turn to whichever one of us picks up the phone if they need a sounding board for general brainstorming. But if it's a matter of finances, health insurance, athletic injuries, vitamins, alternative medicine, animal psychology, or traveling, you talk to Dad.

If you want someone to take a salsa class with you or go Scottish dancing, he's your man. If you are supposed to fly to England tomorrow and your passport has expired, Dad knows what to do and, moreover, he'll drive you (going eighty miles an hour) to the passport office *and* to the airport.

If it's a matter of the heart, an editing request, a question of human psychology, or medical research on just about any health issue, you turn to Mom. If you need an accurate rendering of the past, or a recipe for a tofu meal that can be cooked in less than ten minutes, or a ritual to help your friend get over a breakup, it's Mom who will come through.

Here's the rule of thumb: Dad handles enormous crises that are probably not going to come to pass, but still might; Mom handles the crises that have really happened, and she helps you pick up the pieces. (Then Dad picks up Mom.) Dad helps you plan your whole life; Mom helps you decide what to do right now and suggests what to wear.

If the parent with the requisite skills is away, our daughters know we can understudy for each other and can play out the other's role—and we're not bad at it either. And our daughters know we can function as a unit when it comes to sharing joy, laughter, and sorrow.

Rebecca bids us to see how she and Isaac demonstrate collaborative parenting, and she suggests we can benefit from their approach. Note some of the premises that underlie the way they parent together. Each partner brings distinctive strengths that can be best tapped, given the situation at hand. Each is aware of his or her own strengths and those of the partner. The partners believe in each other's competencies and show respect and admiration for each other's talents, intuitions, and capacities. While sometimes the partners act in concert, they know it is not only useful but sometimes preferable if they take turns. The partners know who ought to step forward, because in the given situation, he or she can be more stable, steady, reliable, and effective. They also know who should step back and take a more supportive role. They know that over a lifetime they will become even more adept at the parenting ballet of stepping back, stepping forward, and sometimes stepping together.

Embracing the Gift of Rebecca

The rainbow is the sign God gives the people of Noah's generation as a gift after the flood. It can be compared to an engagement ring, suggesting that the promise of love is forever. The rainbow is the concrete sign of God's promise to stay in relationship with humanity and to abide by a covenant of love—no matter what. Even after fights, misunderstandings, and disappointments, God is going to be there, forgiving, loving, ready to start all over again. My teacher, Rabbi Yitz Greenberg, once said that a rainbow is a sign of peace because it signals the kinds of limits we need to accept for the sake of healing a broken world.

Rebecca offers a ritual for all adults who collaborate in raising children. That includes parents who are separated or divorced, for as we well know, bringing up children is a lifelong commitment, one not undone by changes in one's marital status. The ritual might also include those people who get involved along the way: godparents, stepparents, foster parents, birth parents, grandparents, aunts, uncles, and close friends.

You need a rainbow to perform Rebecca's ritual, and as the real McCoy, Roy G. Biv in the sky, arrives only serendipitously, and not on demand, you may have to find a crystal prism to create one for yourself. A picture of a rainbow will also suffice, and less literal symbols of rainbows work just as well. Your rainbow could be a picture of your child, or even a picture your child made that you have saved.

You perform Rebecca's ritual whenever you and your partner (or partners) in parenthood have had a misunderstanding, a disappointment, or a failure of the minds to meet about your child. You may have disagreed about where a child will go to school or about whether inoculations are safe. Perhaps you are arguing over whether the issues your child is facing—such as having trouble learning, or being bullied, or not taking school seriously enough, or being anxious—is something that needs to be addressed professionally, or just might go away on its own. You may be struggling to negotiate what faith the child will be raised in, and what holidays will be celebrated. Perhaps you have had a misunderstanding about who was in charge of pick-up, or who was in charge of getting to the doctor's appointment. Maybe it's as large as a custodial battle.

No matter the cause of the disagreement, try performing this ritual to bridge the gap. Meet in the presence of the rainbow you have selected and renew your commitment to find a way to work harmoniously together on behalf of your child. Despite harsh words that may have passed between you, and despite hurts that may have been caused by misunderstandings or insensitivities, reaffirm that you will do whatever is necessary—compromising, calling a truce, seeking mediation and counseling—to place your child's well-being first.

CHAPTER 12

YOCHEVED
LETTING CHILDREN GO

The Biblical Story

Pharaoh charged all his people, saying, "Throw every son that is born into the Nile, but let every girl live."

A man of the house of Levi married a Levite woman. The woman, Yocheved, became pregnant and bore a son, and seeing how beautiful he was, she hid him for three months. When she could hide him no longer, she made a little ark and caulked it with loam and pitch. She put the child in it and placed it among the reeds by the bank of the Nile. The baby's sister, Miriam, stationed herself at a distance, to learn what would happen to him. The daughter of Pharaoh went to bathe at the Nile and spied the little ark among the reeds and sent her maid to fetch it. When she opened it, she saw that it was a child, a boy crying. . . .

Moses's sister approached Pharaoh's daughter, asking, "Shall I go and find you a Hebrew woman to nurse your child for you?" Pharaoh's daughter said, "Yes." Miriam went and called the child's mother. Pharaoh's daughter said to Yocheved, "Take this child and nurse it for me, and I will pay your wages." Yocheved took the child and nursed it. When the child grew up, she brought him to Pharaoh's daughter and he became her son. She named him Moses.

—Adapted from Exodus 1:22–2:10

Yocheved's Own Story

At the edge of the Nile, Yocheved gathered reeds, and exactly as her mother had taught her, she began to weave the basket to hold her baby son. She called him "my son, may God protect you," for she knew she could not give him the name that he would take with him. He would have to wait for the name to be given to him by his own life, by his own loves, and by his own pains, for all this was yet known.

Yocheved split the reed with her nail and tucked it under, securing it under the rows below, then starting again with a new reed. Over, under, over, under, until the basket was strong enough and high enough to hold this precious baby. He was growing so quickly, three months almost, and his cry was getting too loud to muffle. She could not hide him from the soldiers much longer. Yocheved moved her hands automatically. She broke her rhythm only occasionally to arch and bend her back to sooth the baby tied in a blanket across her chest. He became fretful, and she lifted him out and nursed him until he was full and sleepy.

He was not delicate or fine-featured like his sister Miriam or brother Aaron. He was robust, chubby even. In his sleep, he gripped Yocheved's finger, as if he wanted to lead her away from all the suffering and toward a place of freedom and dignity. He was just a baby, and all this presentiment . . .

Yocheved positioned the sleeping baby under the blanket so that his ear rested on her beating heart. She continued to weave as she spoke to her mother in heaven.

"You taught me to weave baskets for my babies so I could place them beside me when they were too large to carry. You never taught me how to make a basket strong enough to hold my child so he might float away from death."

The voice of her mother came to her in the lapping of the water.

"When this child was born, your whole house was filled with light. You had enough love to give birth to him, even though you knew you might not be able to keep him safe forever. In this way, he is no different from all our children. We must release them to the world sooner or later, and pray they will float with enough safety, enough love, and enough happiness through life."

Yocheved's instinct was to make the basket airtight, close as a sarcophagus. But if she did, the baby would perish. He had to be able to breathe and see out, to feel God's presence in the clouds before him and to know he was sealed by the covenant of the rainbow of Noah, peace be upon him. She caulked the basket with clay, until its rounded shape became squared and it looked like a giant brick, the familiar bricks the Hebrew slaves were made to fashion day and night. To cover the basket, she made an arch of white feathers and branches that would let in enough air and light.

On the morning the baby was too large and too loud to survive detection another night in their house, Yocheved swaddled him in her shawl and placed him in his basket. Strong, surprising thoughts came into her mind. This new womb she had made for her baby would allow him to be reborn through the passageway of the river. She willed herself to trust there was a distinctive fate that would unfold for him. One day perhaps her son would go through different waters, and he would lead the enslaved Hebrew people to emerge from the constraints of Egypt, and to be reborn as free people. What mother didn't hold this hope for her child? But maybe this one would. She first had to release him, set him free.

She told herself what she had said to the many women whom she, as a midwife, had assisted in giving birth, when they were losing the strength to push further: "You must. You must deliver this child into the world." Yocheved clutched at her stomach: it was as if she were having contractions once again. "You must."

She had said nothing to Miriam about the basket she had been fashioning, but between her and Miriam, few words were needed. Miriam knew. Together they pulled the basket out from under the branches along the Nile where Yocheved had hidden it. As they worked, Yocheved whispered instructions to Miriam: "Keep your eye on the child, but keep a distance." This was the advice her own mother had given her in less catastrophic times: to guard from afar the ones she loved.

Though Yocheved would have preferred to go on holding her baby forever, she stood at the edge of the water among the reeds, preparing to release him into the world as a gift. "I bless your first journey, my son. May God protect you and be with you," she prayed. "Be safe from harm, open to miracles, and ready to embrace those who love you and challenge you. If God cannot bring you home to me, may you always be warmed and lightened by my love."

With these words, she set him afloat.

Yocheved Speaks to Us

"Let my people go" is the famous refrain of the Exodus story, spoken by Moses to Pharaoh over and over until Pharaoh finally relents. From Moses's mother, Yocheved, we can learn about a different, although related, kind of letting go.

Yocheved teaches us that as much as we are loath to let a child go, we must nonetheless find safe and wise ways to launch our children into the world if they are to survive and flourish as independent, skillful, and competent people. We must equip them with skills for self-protection and tutor them to preserve themselves as they embrace life, full of passion and curiosity. We must, like Pharaoh, let our young beloved people go—otherwise, they become slaves to our love and slaves to our fears. Like Pharaoh, our instincts might be just the opposite, to resist: "No, no, no, I will not let them go!"

Had Yocheved not let her son go at the right time and in the right place and with all the right precautions in place, Moses would surely not have survived infancy. He would not have grown into a man whose own life experiences, growing up in the house of Pharaoh, prepared him to lead his people out of a place of constriction and oppression and into openness and freedom.

Obviously, in a less harsh environment, Yocheved would not have chosen to release Moses into the world as an infant. Pharaoh's decree that the Hebrew baby boys be killed left Yocheved with a single choice. She had to let him float into the world with the hope that he would be rescued by an adoptive parent and flourish.

Sending her son into the world, Yocheved took every precaution. She carefully fashioned a small ark for him, reminiscent of the ark Noah was instructed to make for his family and the animals, which would rescue them all from an evil world and bring them into a new world, under the sign of a rainbow, symbolizing God's protective and enduring covenant.

She lined his little boat with all the protective materials available to her. We do this for our children too, making the protective materials of our world available to them, providing them with immunizations, vitamins, healthful foods, car seats, play spaces, and toys that meet all the safety guidelines.

By placing Moses in the Nile, Yocheved brought him to a place that provided optimal possibilities for his survival. We do this when we carefully choose an obstetrician, midwife, birthing center, or hospital; when we scrutinize the pediatrician who will provide regular exams; when we evaluate preschools—all the way up to choosing a college. We do this when our children bring home their potential life-partners, relying on our gut instincts to imagine if this person can make our child feel loved and happy.

By assigning Miriam, Moses's sister, to keep watch over baby Moses as he floated toward his rescue, Yocheved put her trust in a surrogate to monitor his safety and progress. When we delegate some of the responsibility for our children to others—babysitters, teachers, coaches, counselors, deans, and other mentors—we are doing the same thing. We do it when we supervise our children's progress from the sidelines, knowing when we should keep our distance unless danger requires us to move in.

At every juncture, parents are told it's in the child's best interest for us to find the right times to let go. Especially if we've been raised by parents who may have failed to release us at appropriate times, we think we—by contrast—will have the good sense to know when it's right to let go of our own children. How could we be overprotective ourselves, when we were so constrained by the overprotection of our parents, which kept us from experiencing the fullness of life and from developing our own instincts for competency?

It's not so simple, many of us discover. Demons of past generations tend to slip uninvited into our own psyches, and we find ourselves holding on as tenaciously as our parents did. We may find it easier to justify holding on to a child than to convince ourselves that now is the time to let go. The rationales for holding on seem to grow each day. Our grandparents worried about their children getting lost or getting into car accidents. Our parents worried about sex and drugs. We worry about all those things too, and add to our list sexually transmitted diseases, guns in schools, toxic environments, tainted meat, abduction, sexual abuse, and terrorism. We just want to huddle our little chicks more tightly in the nest.

The first time I was told to let go was when I gave birth to my first child and planned to have a "rooming in" arrangement in which she stayed with me in the hospital instead of in the nursery. After a C-section, after not having slept for many, many hours, the nurses tried to persuade me to keep the baby in the nursery at least for the first couple of days. They told me the best thing I could do for my newborn was to rest, get stronger, and accept the help of trained maternity nurses who actually knew what they were doing. I disagreed—I knew I could do it. This was the first test I had given myself to prove that I was a good mother. Very quickly, I discovered the nurses were right. I had just had major surgery and couldn't even get out of bed, tethered as I was to all kinds of lines. Diapering my baby on the second day of her life had nothing to do with my being a good mother. "I promise you," the nurse said when I asked her to come and bring my baby back to the nursery, "you will have the rest of your life to care for this child."

This has become emblematic of my own parenting style. I start off struggling to let go of my daughters, and then, once I can persuade myself or be persuaded of the inherent good sense of releasing them into the world, I can eventually do so. I try not to let my own fears get out of hand and block their way. I was sorely tested recently. My older daughter, who is training to become an anthropologist, was scheduled to do field work in the Middle East just as the war in Iraq was breaking out. Friends of mine said, "You must forbid her from going." I couldn't quite picture doing that, however much I ached to say, "No! Don't go!" First, she's a young adult who has proven herself capable of making wise decisions, and it's hardly my position anymore to tell her what she can and can't do. Second, she had good reason to go forward with her plans, as her research concerned how people respond to threats of terror. I put my trust in her and she went on the trip, and she did her work safely and professionally. I was very proud of her, and of me, too. When she returned home, I resumed breathing.

Yocheved reminds us that we can't let our own anxieties rob our children of experiences and influences that could fill their lives with light. Martin Buber, author of *Tales of the Hasidim*, retells a story of the

Hasidic teacher called the Baal Shem Tov that captures this elegantly. The Baal Shem Tov once asked his disciple, Rabbi Meir, if he remembered one Sabbath when he was just beginning to study the Torah. Rabbi Meir's father's house was filled with guests, and Meir had been lifted up onto the table so that he could recite all that he had learned. The rabbi certainly remembered. In the middle of his recitation his mother had snatched him down from the table. This annoyed his father, but she pointed to a man at the doorway. He was dressed in sheepskins, like a peasant, and he looked right at her son. Everyone understood it was the evil eye that she feared.

It was then that the Baal Shem Tov revealed to his disciple, "It was I. . . . In such hours a glance can flood the soul with great light. But the fear of men builds walls to keep the light away."[1] Had Rabbi Meir's mother not been so fearful of influences on her son she couldn't contain or control, her son would have found his true mentor that much earlier.

The story of Yocheved has an important ending. Not long after Yocheved says her heart-wrenching good-bye to her baby, the daughter of Pharaoh rescues him. Miriam, who has been watching out for him, shows up, offering to find a woman to nurse the baby. Yocheved is then hired to nurse him and raise him until he is old enough to return to the house of his rescuer. Yocheved, thus, offers insight for contemporary parents who have become empty nesters. The nest, she tells us, may indeed be officially empty, but our baby birds have a tendency to return, looking for advice, encouragement, and nostalgic replays of family routines. For their own sakes, once we have provided our children with what they came for, we must help them get back to their own journeys.

Embracing Yocheved's Gift

Most cultures have rituals, symbolic behaviors that give one a sense of order, that help parents release their children into the world. Some rituals come near birth: both circumcision and baptism serve as signs made on the body of the baby to denote spiritual protection. Other rituals take place at puberty, and if they involve hunting, going off on a quest or journey, or recitation of the group's sacred teachings, they signify—

to us, to our community, and to our children—that our children have the right skills to move on as mature persons.

We find ourselves seeking rituals of letting go that will strengthen our children and us, too, when we send them to school for the first time, when they go off on summer adventures, when they leave for college. Even when they go off for the day and depart from our presence, we seek a ritual to imprint our protective wishes on them until their safe return. We say, "Good-bye" meaning, "God be with you"; we say, "Drive safely and buckle up"; we say, "Call when you get there." These words of departure are not just about conveying information. They are miniceremonies of protection.

Rituals of departure let us know that we have done everything necessary and everything possible on behalf of our children's safety, and now it's time to release them in good conscience. Such rituals help us contain our anxieties, goad us to provide our children with the right skills at each juncture, and give us a way to make the break. As our children become older and more aware, rituals of departure let them know that we have confidence that they will make wise and safe choices and that wherever they go in the world without us, our blessing rests with them.

We can well imagine that as Yocheved placed Moses in his little ark, she sent him off with a prayer, expressing her wish that she be able to let go and that he be protected. Many parents have evolved practices for letting go, practices that emerge naturally out of the routines of every day and some that have been passed on. Consider this ritual that anthropologist Gina Bria devised when her children started school. She calls it a "morning exit rite":

> *The last stop at the door, usually reserved for collar pulls and hair straightening, was transformed when I simply pressed my hand on their heads. "I'm sending you out to the world; come back safe." My children would return for that benediction if I had forgotten it. . . . I've caught my three-year-old saying good-bye to his older sister. He reaches up and puts his hand on her brow, often leaving behind a peanut-butter smear. "Yuck" she yells, but she exits knowing she will return to a haven.*[2]

To let go, as Yocheved did, there is an ancient blessing, adapted here, that you can say for yourself as you release your child into the world: "Blessed are You who prepares me to release my child."

Bestow your version of this ancient blessing upon your child at times of parting: "May God bless you and protect you all the days of your life and give you peace."

For a particularly significant departure, you might want to give your child something that serves as a protective amulet, symbolizing your love and instructions for safety. At such a time, you might offer to give your child a necklace, a ring, or even a hat he or she has seen you wear and identifies with you—something that can serve as a sign of your loving protection when you are not there. Some of my Christian students say that when they left for college, their parents gave them crosses to wear, and they have not taken them off. In many Jewish families, children going off to college are given their own mezuzah, an amulet for the door that holds scripture inside. Seeing the mezuzah each time they cross the threshold, they are reminded that as they go in and out of the world, they must maintain the precious, life-sustaining values they were raised to uphold.

In praying for the well-being of our own children as we release them into the world, we realize our hearts are merged with those of all parents. The feeling of collective worry, but more important, the collective responsibility we—along with God—have for all children who have been allowed to float free, like Moses, into the world, is captured in the Reverend Meg Riley's prayer:

Rushing river of days,
Cradle every parent's child in your waters.

We launch our babes in fragile baskets,
Moses multiplied by millions, released from muddy shores.

We squint to see around your bends
As our hearts are carried away.
We toss small sticks to float behind baskets, our prayers.[3]

PART V

HEALING

CHAPTER 13

THE WOMAN WHO HAS GIVEN BIRTH
WAITING FOR THE RIGHT TIME

The Biblical Story

The Lord said to Moses, "Tell the people of Israel, if a woman conceives, and bears a male child, then she shall be unclean seven days; as at the time of her menstruation, she shall be unclean. On the eighth day the flesh of his foreskin shall be circumcised. She shall continue for thirty-three days in the blood of her purifying; she shall not touch any hallowed thing, nor come into the sanctuary, until the days of her purifying are completed. But if she bears a female child, then she shall be unclean two weeks, as in her menstruation; and she shall continue in the blood of her purifying for sixty-six days. When the days of her purifying are completed, whether for a son or for a daughter, she shall bring to the priest at the door of the Tent of Meeting a lamb a year old for a burnt offering, and a young pigeon or a turtledove for a sin offering, and he shall offer it before the Lord and make atonement for her; then she shall be clean from the flow of her blood. This is the law for her who bears a child, either male or female. If she cannot afford a lamb, then she shall take two turtledoves or two young pigeons, one for a burnt offering and the other for a sin offering; and the priest shall make atonement for her, and she shall be clean.

—Adapted from Leviticus 12:1–8

The Woman Who Has Given Birth's Own Story

She—the woman who has just given birth to a son; she—the woman who has just given birth to a daughter—she was breathless, she was exhilarated as her child was placed into her arms. A son or a daughter? It didn't matter which to her; the baby was alive, and she was, too. Its being a girl or boy mattered deeply to others, particularly the midwife who had, for weeks before, dangled a coin on a string over her belly, making predictions and changing them. For the woman, the birth alone satisfied the large and important curiosities she carried for nine months. Would she be capable of this majestic feat of carrying a baby and pushing it into life? What would the pain feel like? Would all her anticipation for this moment be turned against her, and would the audacity of expecting a miracle mock her optimism with a disappointment? What would her husband feel? Would he love the baby enough, and love her more, too?

Such a flood of feelings! The baby she held in her hands was all wonder, a miracle. She pressed the child to her cheeks, to her eyes, and she drank in the baby's presence. She asked herself in disbelief, "Could this baby have really come from me?" She heard a loud, squawking cry, as strong and willful as a new bird. The baby was alive, well, and breathing. She could see the baby had all the right parts, even features that could be traced, if you used your imagination, to both mother and father, satisfying the vanities of both sides. She who had given birth vowed from her heart: "I will never forget this moment. I will never forget the intensity of the joy. And I will never forget being ripped apart with blades of fire from inside me. How could any woman ever, ever do this again?"

The other women—her midwife, mother, sisters, and friends—had all said, meaning to prepare her, that giving birth would hurt. But they didn't say anything about how much. This omission shocked her. Why had they only used the word *pain*? Say better: "stabbing pain that exceeds anything you could imagine, pain that requires heroism and courage, pain that is like mortal combat." She felt the women had betrayed her by holding back the truth. But what if they *had* spoken the truth, and she had not listened to them, thinking she was the exceptional woman, being braver, more vigorous, less dainty and prone to complain?

"Now you must feed the child!" the women attending her commanded, calling her "Mother," as if addressing her by this new name could transform her from the person she had always been before into a new one. "I am not a mother," she said to herself. "I am myself, with a baby." "What about me? Where did I go? Am I a person only in relationship to this baby?"

She had just been through the most arduous experience of her life, and she was proud she had come through it. How could they be telling her to put a crying baby to her breast to feed *now*? She wanted only to sleep, to be cradled in her husband's arms. Once she was well rested, maybe then she'd be ready to take care of a baby. Would being a mother to this child always feel like too gigantic a responsibility, as it did at this moment? If so, was it too late to escape, to change her mind?

The baby would not latch onto her breast. "What if I can't teach this baby how to eat to stop its hunger?" Forgetting that babies come with wise instincts and that they learn from life, she worried: "What if I fail to teach the baby everything needed to survive: to walk, to speak, to love?" She spun out a lifetime of disasters, and in her inattentiveness, the baby latched on and sucked ferociously to sleep.

For all that she had been through, there was no ceremony she could perform immediately to mark the enormity she had experienced. Just waiting. Several weeks after having a son, and even longer after a daughter. As she had waited through the months of pregnancy, she would wait again. She waited the requisite weeks. Her body began to look and feel more familiar. Her child nursed adeptly and slept with some predictability. With surprising speed, her memory of every part of giving birth, except for the blissful astonishment of receiving her child into her arms, grew less vivid. She was beginning to forget why (or even if) she had vowed never to give birth again. She was regaining hold of who she was. Yes, she was the mother, and she now turned when called by that name. But she was also a version of her former self. When the time had come for her to immerse in the fresh waters of the ritual bath and to bring an offering of turtledoves to the temple, she was ready to mark the process of healing that had—almost on its own—already begun.

The Woman Who Has Given Birth Speaks to Us

Most cultures offer ritual responses to life-changing events, such as childbirth, that leave us, at the moment of the event and long beyond it, astonished, overwhelmed, emotionally swamped, and unsure of who we are and of what is going to happen next.

In Leviticus, we learn about practices women were to follow after giving birth. If the woman had given birth to a son, she was to be considered "impure" for a period of seven days. (A woman's bleeding for a period of several days after giving birth constituted what was considered a state of spiritual impurity for the biblical community, comparable to the impurity caused by a man's seminal emission.) Consequently, she was not permitted to enter the sanctuary to make sacrifices or to touch sacred vessels. She and her husband were not permitted to have physical contact with each other. She was to wait thirty-three more days. At that point, she bathed in a ritual bath and was considered purified, ready to resume both her spiritual and her sexual lives. The birth of a daughter would render her impure for two weeks, and she was to wait an additional sixty-six days before immersing in the ritual bath. She would then bring an offering to the temple. She would thank God for having kept her alive through childbirth and for having given her this child. She would ask God to protect her newborn.

We can encounter the woman who has given birth, whether to a son or to a daughter, as someone who represents all women giving birth. We meet her at an extremely vulnerable point in her life: from the time she gives birth to a period several weeks later. An experience that has been painful, frightening, joyous, wonderful, and disorienting has changed her life. Notice how her culture would have her mark this event: by *not* marking it immediately. She must wait to give ceremonial shape to her experiences.

"What about baby-welcoming ceremonies?" you may ask. "Don't they mark pregnancy and childbirth?" Such ceremonies do mark a child's entering a family and a community and give parents occasion to express gratitude and pray for help, but they focus only on the happy conclusion of the last nine months, and not on the woman's personal experience of having carried a baby, giving birth, and becoming a mother.

The woman who has given birth asks us to see the wisdom of waiting before officially marking an experience. She acknowledges that we may first need to confront aspects of the biblical postpartum practices that seem so incompatible with modern sensibilities. The biblical practices appear to view the new mother as impure, a source of contamination needing to be contained, lest she pollute others. They suggest man's fear of female bodies, both their effluvia and their life-giving power. And why should giving birth to a girl require a longer wait? Is this the old story of a culture kicking up its heels upon the birth of boys, seen as assets, and rolling its eyes upon the birth of daughters, seen as burdens?

Those who uphold the ancient practice, which continues (minus the sacrifices) in some communities, would want it understood that the new mother's impurity is not about her being physically gross or disgusting. Rather, it's about a temporary spiritual state: she is, in the lingo of ritual studies, "betwixt and between." Besides, they might add, the idea of refraining from intercourse after childbirth is medically wise; most obstetricians prescribe a period of several weeks' abstinence until enough healing has taken place. Many new mothers would say that as much as they might, in principle, be eager to resume sexual relations, both physically and psychically, they're happy enough not to rush in.

Whether or not we can cordon off our objections to potentially troubling aspects of the ancient practice, the woman who gives birth asks us to see the virtues of a ritual that begins with an extensive waiting period. She tells us that we don't need to give closure to *any* big, transformative experience of our lives just for the sake of moving on efficiently. Beyond childbirth, there are many times when we would do better to wait, taking time to make sense of what has happened and to allow our bodies and minds to feel whole again.

In waiting, a new mother can slowly integrate the experiences of pregnancy and giving birth: the shock and thrill of standing on the threshold of being a parent and the anxiety of sustaining a child. She is not forced to process the experience too quickly. She can slowly acknowledge that something big has happened in her life, but she doesn't have to tie it up neatly with meaning before she is ready.

There is wisdom behind all rituals that begin with waiting. I call them "rituals of repression." The belatedness of such rituals helps us to absorb experiences that are simply too large to handle consciously and publicly at the moment. They keep us from having to integrate what has happened before we are ready. They allow us to not get back into the swing of things prematurely. They keep us from pretending, for the sake of others, that we have bounced back to our former selves, when in fact, in the process of waiting, we are becoming someone new.

Giving birth, for a mother, is a huge and overwhelming psychic and physical experience, wherever it's done—at home, in a bath of warm water, in a cozy suite in a birthing center, in a hospital with beeping fetal monitors. Consider these reflections by Rabbi Dianne Cohler-Esses, now the mother of three, on the birth of her first child:

> . . . *it was I that broke open at birth. The sea opened at birth and though the sea closed again, it swirled and gushed ceaselessly, as if to make up for having to split, payback for having to stand painfully rigid for an eternal moment, the eternity required for my firstborn daughter to enter from the timeless womb into this mercilessly temporal world. Soon after her birth, with the flow of my milk also came the flood of my tears each day at the time of the sun's dissolution into darkness, threatening to drown mother and child both. Some called it postpartum depression. Looking back, however, I call it the death of an autonomous woman, the death of a woman for the sake of the creation of a child and her mother.[1]*

Note how waiting for a number of weeks before immersing in a ritual bath was as helpful for Dianne as it was for the biblical woman who has given birth. Dianne reflects:

> *Some months after my daughter was born, I began to wake from this watery dream, from this strange and double-edged Edenic fusion. I woke to hear calls and cries from life beyond my baby. I can't tell you when it happened. All I know is I started to yearn for life beyond fusion. I had enough of enclosing circles, enough of my body flowing endlessly into hers. I began to feel threatened, as if my boundaries would dissolve entirely and once and for all. And, after all, I still did have a distinct body and mind, as hard as it was at that time to discern them as separate entities. Now I wanted the definition of my body to return;*

I wanted to recall the life of my mind; I wanted echoes of my previous existence, my stolen mobility and autonomy returned. When I search through that watery time for the time of an actual event, I conclude that it must have been after the biblically mandated two months when I decided to go to the mikvah *[the Jewish ritual bath]. But, to tell you the truth, I'm not sure. I went to reclaim my body and self in a pool of living water, the very water in which, becoming a mother, I lost myself. I thought that the healing required would come, so to speak, from the wound itself. I believed the ritual bath, with its attendant birth imagery, would provide for the passage out of the water, would provide a rebirth back into distinction, a return to solid existence, to my own identity, beyond the mythic animal realm of the nurturing mother. Water would meet water and thus I would be reborn into distinction. . . . The experience was . . . a marker in the muddiness of growth and change. It marked the point at which I decided to reach for something else, the point at which I wanted once more to become identifiable, mobile, separate, apart (for longer intervals) from my child. . . . It was my attempt to enter the water in order to emerge from it. It wasn't that I wanted never to return to the gentle dissolving of boundaries that water represented, but that I wanted the power to enter and emerge from the water again and again, choosing water or air or solids depending on what was required in that moment. Now lines would slowly return to my life and intersect with the great circles of life and death. I could, again, be a teacher and creator in the larger world, I could forge connections beyond my family, I could go out and I could return. And that ability to go out into the world and return to my family became, in itself, a new source of joy.*[2]

The woman who has given birth wants us to see that rituals of repression come into play when life hands us an event, or a string of events—good or bad—that is so large and overwhelming that all we can do is note, "Something really big, powerful, and complicated has happened," without being able to frame it or to give it precise meaning at the moment.

Many people mistrust repression, even if it is just an initial step along the way toward healing. When something truly horrible happens in the United States—a terrorist attack, a shooting spree in a school—the standard procedure has been to send in a team of therapists or clergy specially trained in trauma (in the military, they are sometimes called "casualty assistance technicians") to help the surviving victims, their families, the rescuers, even traumatized bystanders. To fend off repression, the experts typically encourage the psychically wounded to tell their stories, to experience the trauma anew, and to feel all the feelings once more. The theory is that the more immediately and more deeply one processes the trauma, the better—maybe even the more efficiently—one is healed. The trauma team might help the victims to anticipate adverse responses, such as feeling as though they are reliving the traumatic event, having nightmares or flashbacks, or feeling numb and unable to function normally. They are warned to anticipate symptoms of post-traumatic stress disorder even if at the moment, they are feeling emotionally stable and under control.

This protocol is being challenged. Researchers are noting that many people who have suffered trauma (such as a disaster, an attack, or a serious accident) and then have gone on to spring back have often *avoided* the ministration of the trauma teams. Usually they are described as having resilient personalities. They choose *not* to relive the experience and its emotions, wading through the horror of it all again. Instead, they are said to have chosen (using the abundant cache of clichés that exist to discuss such things) "to sweep it under the rug," "to pull themselves up by their bootstraps" and not "to wallow in the past" and preferred instead "to get on with it." In other words, even while they could have been embraced by experts leaping to assist them, they chose to fend off offers of intervention so that they could attend to their wounds and memories in their own time and in their own way. Is it a coincidence that they have healed without consciously processing the trauma? Or is their healing a *result* of their having chosen temporary repression over speedy process? In the area of the study of trauma, this remains an open debate.

In everyday interactions, repression clearly has its place. Employees who have issues with their bosses are, in fact, repressing their negative feelings when they resist acting out their anger and choose not tell their bosses off. They are said to be acting "professionally" when they choose to move beyond anger, even forgetting it, especially when dealing with an issue that can't be resolved or with a coworker with an impossible personality. And consider how repression works for people in sales or in the arts who get rejections all the time. Were they to process each rejection—each pair of shoes that was tried on and went unsold, each role they auditioned for and didn't get, each canvas that was passed over by the Whitney Museum—they would probably be swamped in self-doubt and give up. Repressing the response to rejection and taking it in one's stride make it possible to keep putting oneself out there.

The choice to address trauma head-on by either processing the event and its subsequent emotions or by repressing it for a while is likely to be driven by one's personality as much as it is by the life situations that come our way. Some people are moved to relive a troubling experience in the presence of a caring other and find healing in doing so, and that's the right path for them. For others, this is yet another nightmare to endure. "It was bad enough the first time around," some say. "Don't make me go through it all over again. I'll heal in my own time." Anthropologist Robert F. Murphy, who became disabled, explains that his strategy for calmly living day to day in the face of uncertain health was "to block from my consciousness any thoughts about the final outcome of the illness, to repress from awareness any vision of the unthinkable."[3]

The woman who has given birth reminds us that we can choose to process big events at our own pace, even if that means we plan to take a good long while. I share the story of an undergraduate who was inspired by the story of the woman who has given birth. Her story gave this young woman the confidence to feel that her choice to react to her parents' recent divorce in her own time and in her own way was legitimate:

> *My mother wanted me to go into therapy after she and my father got divorced in my senior year in high school. It came out of the blue, at least for me, although I suppose I should have read the signs. My mother was right that I was shocked. It was calamitous having my family fall apart just as I was about to go away to college. (Thanks, parents, good timing. Did you really think this would make it easier for me?) But I wasn't going to talk about it with some stranger at the psych*

counseling center just to soothe my mother's conscience, and it's not that I haven't been in therapy before. I have my own inner calendar, and just because my parents picked this time to break up, since it was convenient for them, it doesn't mean I have to make sense of it all just now. It's enough to be a college freshman and deal with having a roommate and how to structure my time. I'll process my parents' divorce when I'm ready to, and it's not now, thank you. Does that mean I'm repressing the whole business? Maybe, but who says repressing is such a bad thing if it's what I need to do? I want to be pissed and confused and I want to wallow in it all and dread going home for Thanksgiving and feel really sorry for myself. I will not stop whining and have it all neatly tied up—which is what my mother wants me to do because then she'd feel less guilty about what she's done to me. I'll be the one to decide when I'm ready.

The readiness to process comes when we're ready. I used to feel so annoyed when my daughters' daycare teachers would forget my name and call me "Julie and Elizabeth's mother," as if that was the whole of who I was. Now, when I'm at a conference and a former classmate of my older daughter's says, "Excuse me, but you're Julie's mother, aren't you?" or if I'm at the farmer's market and children my younger daughter used to babysit for come up to me and wave, saying, "Hi, Elizabeth's mother!" as if I were Snow White at Disneyland, I tend to feel not only that I've been correctly identified, but quite famous indeed.

It only took about fifteen years.

Embracing the Gift of the Woman Who Has Given Birth

Some rituals immediately help process and shape what's going on in your life. At times these are exactly the right rituals you need to perform. A wedding ceremony takes your love and commitment to each other and, with the exchange of documents, rings, and vows, translates that immediately, dramatically, and publicly into your being married. Graduation, with the declaration of the college president and the toss of the tassel on your cap, turns you into a graduate.

Other rituals give us formal, acceptable ways to postpone dealing immediately with what's at hand, and allow us to make meaning in our own time. The event needn't be a negative one: it could be a change for the good that has an enormous impact on us. Consider, for example, moving to a new house in a new place. There are good reasons many of us take the month-long grace period we're given when we move to a new state until we make our new residence official by getting a new driver's license and license plates. We'll wait a number of weeks before holding a housewarming party, and it's not only because we need time to unpack. We need time to feel that the house we're living in has become our own.

When we perform the ritual of the woman who has given birth, after any big event, we wait. We resist processing our lives according to someone else's timetable. We assure ourselves we're neither being lazy nor failing to accept reality. We anticipate a time of closure will come. (We also listen to the people who know us best when they tell us that our waiting puts our families or us at risk. It is not a good idea, for example, for a new mother who is struggling with an extended postpartum depression to wait for time to heal: she and her family deserve medical help.)

With these words from Ecclesiastes 3:1 in mind, you can begin your waiting period: "For everything there is a season, and a time and purpose for every matter under heaven."

Then make an informal contract with yourself, noting when you might create a private ceremony that allows you to put closure to the time of your waiting, and how you might wish to mark your transformation and healing.

CHAPTER 14

JOB'S WIFE
HEALING BY EXPRESSING ANGER

The Biblical Story

Job's sons and daughters were eating and drinking wine in the house of their eldest brother when suddenly a mighty wind came from the wilderness. It struck the four corners of the house so that it collapsed upon the young people and they died.

Job arose, tore his robe, cut off his hair, and threw himself on the ground and worshipped. He said, "Naked I came from my mother's womb and naked shall I return. The Lord has given and the Lord has taken away. Blessed be the name of the Lord."

For all that, Job did not sin or curse God.

. . . Job was inflicted with a severe inflammation from the sole of his foot to the crown of his head. He scratched himself with a potsherd as he sat in ashes.

His wife said to him, "You still keep your integrity! Curse God and die!"

But he said to her, "You talk as any shameless woman might. Should we accept only good from God and not evil?"

For all that, Job said nothing sinful. . . .

. . . Job then said,

"I cry out to you, but you do not answer me. . . .
I looked forward to good fortune, but evil came,
I looked for light, but darkness came."

—Adapted from Job 1:18–22; 2:7–10; 30:20, 26

Job's Wife's Own Story

"I made you some ointment, Job," said his wife. She had pounded camphor and wintergreen leaves together into a paste and offered it to him as he lay limp under a skeleton of a tree in the hot sun. Had morning come? She and Job hardly noticed the movements of light and dark, days and nights into weeks. Grief had pushed them outside the coherent way one keeps track of one's time on earth. They were just there, still alive but numb. Bodies, marking places for souls that were once there. Once strangers to grief, she and Job now inhabited the arid and narrow land of endless sorrow. Only in the strictest sense had they survived the horrific deaths of all their children.

"No ointment," Job said, pushing her away by turning his neck stiffly in the other direction, wrapping himself more rigidly in remnants of a robe the color of dust. "The hurt is beyond hurting; I drown in loss."

At one time she could comfort him with a glance, a touch. Now, nothing. How tiny were the scratches and disappointments they once considered calamities: a finger scalded in cooking, a daughter who took a spill, a son who shrieked with night fears, a wilting barley crop, a sheep or two failing to flourish, a donkey with a sprain. Such were the bumps that had interrupted their constant flow of happiness.

They had believed that those who lived lives of impeccable righteousness, who worked hard at inspecting themselves for imperfections, and who remembered to atone with sincerity, would find favor in God's eyes. Until now, their lives of scrupulous piety and bounteous blessing confirmed their assumption.

Job drew no insight from the fire he burned in now. In an instant, a wind had come and taken all they had and loved. On a single morning, they buried each one of their children, absence piling on absence. Their home gone, their animals, their crops, their health . . . But after the death of the children, the other losses only gave shade to pitch black.

"It would stop the itching," Job's wife said, scooping some of the cool salve into her fingers, remembering how she would do this for the children when the sun had burned them. "I would feel I had at least done something. That's all there is left, Job, that some feeling could stir between us. With no more caring, how will we know we are alive?"

He pushed her fingers away with the back of his palm. "This is the difference between you and me. You can still feel." He struggled to rise to his feet, imagining he had the strength to lift himself and say his morning benedictions. He wilted back to the ground.

"I'll tell you what the difference is between us," his wife said. "You've become a cold stone who continues to pray to the One who spoke and brought the world into being, saying, 'Thank you, thank you.' You're a fool, Job. Can a man pray when he cannot even feel? Your faithfulness is mocked. God shouldn't be hearing your thanks. For what?"

"This is our way. There are no other words but the ancient ones," said Job.

"No, Job. There is no more way, not as we knew it," said his wife. "The old words lost their power when our lives fell apart. You should hear yourself. Your old words, Job, are dead rocks. They don't rise up. We have nothing left to sacrifice, Job, nothing to give to the poor."

"There is still repentance," Job offered.

"Repentance for what? For leading good lives, for raising fine children, for caring for others? For pious worship? Listen to me, Job."

"I will not curse God," he said.

"Curse with God, Job, as I have done. Curse along with God. Could God not also curse the fate that has befallen us?"

Job unleashed his anger. He lashed out at God, at life. His wife waited at a distance as he raged. If God could hear these new words and respond, Job might return to her and to the land of the living.

Job's Wife Speaks to Us

We know little about Job's wife from the biblical text. It offers but a single conversation that she has with her husband. Yet from that wisp of information, in the context of the rest of the story, we can intuit how Job's wife experienced the trials that befell them both. More importantly, Job's wife reveals how she coped and how she then counseled her husband to begin the process of his own healing. As a consequence, she reveals how they were both able to break down the fortresses of isolation that had kept them from finding comfort in each other.

We know a good deal about Job. He is the pious, wealthy man who loses everything. God, provoked by the forces of evil, agrees to test Job to see if Job loves God simply because his life has gone so swimmingly well. What would happen if Job were to lose everything: his children, his home, his prosperity, and his health? We know that despite all the suffering Job endures and the bitterness he feels, he holds out on cursing God for a long time. Only after his wife goads him on does he curse the day he was born.

There is an eventual happy ending for Job. God rebukes Job at great length for having expressed outrage and for having questioned the ways of God. Essentially, God says, "Who do you think you are?" Then, seemingly out of nowhere, God rewards Job with a lottery-like jackpot: fourteen thousand sheep, six thousand camels, one thousand oxen, and one thousand asses, as well as seven sons and three daughters (presumably brand-new ones to replace the ten who died). Job gets to live to the ripe old age of one hundred and forty and see four generations of children and grandchildren.

Was God rewarding Job for his constancy? Not according to Job's wife. She believes God was rewarding them for the courage and integrity they showed when they took God on. I suspect that she reaches this conclusion based on the extremely fine fate her new daughters receive, which must have given her great vicarious pleasure. The new daughters of Mr. and Mrs. Job, unlike their mother and new brothers who all remain anonymous, are dignified with lovely proper names: Jemimah, Keziah, and Kerren-Happuch (meaning, respectively, Dove, Cinnamon, and Eye-Shadow Holder). We are told they are the most beautiful maidens in the land. Unlike other women of their time, these exceptionally fortunate daughters inherit property, just as their brothers do. In one legend, the daughters are said to possess golden sashes that give them the power to speak the language of angels. Is it surprising that the daughters of a woman who spoke articulately and honestly before God would be gifted, themselves, with the capacity to communicate?

Job's wife offers us the same set of constructive, healing responses to suffering that she offered her husband. Do not blame yourself, she tells us, when it's not your fault. Do not stifle your anger, and do not get stuck in it either, fixating on bygones, for it will get you nowhere.

Express your dismay and disappointment. Allow time to heal your wounds. Repairing what can be repaired, reenter the land of the living.

When bad things happen to you or those you care about, it is normal to question and challenge long-held beliefs. It is normal to want to curse God when grief, sadness, disappointment, or unbearable pressures lead you to ask, "Why me?" It is normal to feel angry with God, to feel abandoned. Often, such instincts get suppressed because they seem to be forbidden; at the very least, we think it's not nice to have such feelings. But suppression can leave us, as Melissa Weintraub has written, "fixated on . . . loss, frozen in the posture of grief, . . . closed to the possibility that . . . [one's] devastating reality could change."[1]

Job's wife has observed that all the pious behaviors of her household—the ritual meals, the burnt offerings, and the purification practices Job made his family engage in—have failed to shield them from tragedy. Her faith has been challenged, and well it should be. (Virginia Woolf concurs. In her diary, she wrote that after reading the Book of Job, she came to this conclusion: "I do not think God comes well out of it.")

Job's wife keeps her faith when she understands that in order to go on, she must rage. She trusts God rages along with her.

What does Job's wife say? She has observed what has happened to Job and is outraged that he continues to bless God. While God may be impressed with Job's so-called integrity under duress, his wife does not endorse his stance. How can you sit there, she asks, and accept what has happened, even seeing the good in it, or assuming you are being punished for some sin you haven't performed? What's dignified and pious about your response? Stop rationalizing what has happened to you when no rationale exists. Stop finding excuses for God. You can do better than this, Job, she says. Even if you die, maintain your integrity, your capacity to have a genuine response. Be courageous and honest; let God hear your active voice of outrage. Don't be graceful and gentlemanly. Make waves. Screech your heart out. Demand that goodness be rewarded. Worship God with your honesty.

To better understand the strategy of Job's wife, biblical scholar Ilana Pardes refers us to the Septuagint, an ancient expansion of the biblical texts. There, Job's wife asks her husband how much longer can he go on enduring suffering and waiting for salvation. "Look," she tells him, "your memory is already blotted out from the earth, along with our sons and daughters, and the travail and pangs of my womb, whom I reared in toil for nothing. And you sit in wormy decay, passing the nights in the open, while I roam and drudge from place to place and from house to house, waiting for the sun to go down so that I may rest from my toils and the griefs which now grip me."[2]

If humans have a covenantal partnership with God, and if God needs human help and input in maintaining and bettering the world, then, according to Job's wife, it behooves God to listen up and hear the voice of human collaborators who offer correctives.

Timing is important. Job's wife leads her husband to challenge God and to talk back when he is ready to do so. And Job takes his time.

Job initially rejects his wife's wisdom. He hushes her, telling her she speaks like a shameful woman. While good advice is always hard to heed when it challenges our assumptions and requires us to act against the grain, many—like Job—find wisdom coming from a woman especially hard to accept. ("Don't you think we should ask for directions?" I ask my husband when we are lost. "No! I have to trust my instincts," he says, until he realizes he has driven twenty miles in the wrong direction.) Culture conspires in promulgating this attitude: male wisdom is dignified with the elegant name "The Ethics of the Fathers," even when the advice dispensed ("Who is rich? He who is content with what he has" or "Say little, but do much") is fairly obvious. The precise sources of male wisdom are typically remembered: Hillel, Aristotle, Shakespeare, Jefferson, Einstein, Gandhi. Women's advice, which usually comes down to us unattributed, is further denigrated by the name it is often given: "old wives' tales."

Wise women are still unheeded. This goes on in the business world every day—in boardrooms, corporations, and not-for-profit organizations. Lynn Schusterman, a major philanthropist and a powerful woman to encounter, remarked that when she once brought an idea to the attention of a board meeting of a major charitable organization, it went unnoticed. "But it took a man to say, 'I'm backing her up and if you don't, I'm walking' for others to review the idea."[3] Many women who have desired to promote an agenda or introduce a new idea or practice in an organization will tell you that they first had to stack the room with men who would support the idea in order for the group to listen to it, let alone to take it seriously and adopt it. Women who have cared more about pushing a new policy forward than claiming credit for it will tell you they were successful because they decided to give a man with power in the organization the illusion that their proposal was, in fact, his own good idea. Many Japanese women who own their own businesses have found it necessary to bring male colleagues with them to meetings with customers who are willing to make eye contact only with the men, assuming they have power, while their female bosses do not.[4]

For Job to hear his wife's wisdom, he first must (according to Pardes) "undergo various pious phases of awakening before he can call into question the system of beliefs he has cherished for so long."[5] Then Job can finally curse God by wishing that he had never been born.

After Job opens up to God, he can also open up to his wife. Until then, they have been separated in their grief, so angry at what fate has dealt them that they can hardly comfort each other. They are doubly pained. Not only do they have all these losses, but they have lost the connection to each other as well, so wrapped up are they in their private experiences of grief, their private strategies of holding themselves together. As the legend has it, Job's wife needs to go house to house for consolation: she can find none in her own home, from her most intimate of others, the one who should know exactly how she is feeling. At a time when husband and wife could feel so close and be so supporting, they are as distant as can be. They are two people in the same fix who cannot experience each other's dilemma.

People respond in various ways to the bad things that happen.

Some try to see the bad events as keys that can open up the possibility for better situations yet to come. One ancient Jewish teaching proposes that just as we bless God when good things happen, we ought to bless God when bad things happen. How could this be? The answer is that we never know just how our lives are going to turn out in the long run. The flood that, in the short run, appears to create a calamity, may eventually be the source of a fertile plain that allows for successful agriculture. The fall that caused Grandma to break her ankle and stay in the hospital ends up being the reason her grandson—who came to visit her—met and fell in love with the lovely young intern who was taking care of her (a true story—I was at the wedding!). Thus, we are counseled to bear trials and disappointments and bless the clouds hanging over us for the hidden silver linings that they could contain; we are supposed to look beyond all closed doors for the more propitious open doors that lie ahead.

Some respond with gratitude for their lot. They are the ones who say your bad-case scenario could have been an even worse case scenario. "You ought to thank God that you were in a car accident and only totaled your car and broke two ribs. Look how lucky you were! Imagine: it could have been worse. You could have broken your legs too! You could have died!" These are the people who say that while they would rather not have had emergency open-heart surgery or lung cancer, these medical crises led them to take better care of themselves and value the preciousness of life.

A good many people respond by saying, "God gives us only what we can bear." They shoulder their suffering with grace, finding meaning in it, assuming there may be some lesson they must learn, some divine rationale that they may or may not eventually discern.

Job's wife is satisfied by none of these strategies for facing adversity, however spiritually rich and nurturing they might be for some. She tells her husband: "I cannot accept that this is God's plan. And if it is God's plan, it is still not acceptable. Let's stop finding excuses and rationales." She blessed God in adversity by her honest anger.

When Job and his wife convey their anger to God, they do not erase God from their lives. The opposite is true. Together, they acknowledge what Job's wife intuited initially: God cannot fix all human suffering. God is not responsible for all suffering. God's inability to fix doesn't represent an inability to care. God witnesses our suffering and feels our unbearable pain alongside us.

Job and his wife express their anger, and for this perhaps counterintuitive expression of faithfulness, they are rewarded. They are built up again in family, material possessions, and faith. Not only does their house fill with children, but siblings and former friends come and break bread at their table and offer consolation, comfort, even gold rings. This suggests that the capacity to curse, an emotional response that emerges when piety and critical thinking intersect (yes, that is possible!), can sustain not only one's psyche, but the social order as well. As the individual heals, the family and community heal too.

Job's wife encourages you to give God a piece of your mind. Speaking the truth when what you have to say isn't nice shouldn't weaken your faith. It should sustain and, if necessary, transform it, for it has kept the conversation—which might have been shut down—open. The alternative would be to cease conversation altogether, to hang up on God. That's the dark, lonely place you don't want to be.

Some cultures romanticize those who suffer in silence. Many Americans still hold up Jackie Kennedy, frozenly composed under her black veil at her husband's funeral, as the model of elegant grief to which we ought to aspire. But in other cultures, people do not conceal their grief when the design of their lives unravels. They are encouraged to be expressive and dramatic in their grieving: to shriek, rage, wail, beat one's breast, tear one's clothes, keen. To exhibit restraint would be considered inhuman, a sign of an inability to feel and care.

If, for instance, you and other family members are joined in shouldering the burdens of caring for a sick relative, or if you and others are enduring the grief of a gripping loss or disappointment, you may still feel that not one other person really understands what you yourself are going through. For every poignant magazine article that portrays misfortune or grief as the trigger that brings people together, there is a real-life scenario in which crisis separates people farther and farther. I know my students have a similar feeling when they are, as they say, "freaking out" because of the pressure of exams and papers or because of their anxiety about what to do with the rest of their lives, especially as graduation approaches. They may know, consciously, that most of their classmates are in very much the same place as they are, but that doesn't alleviate their own lonely panic.

Job's wife advises that when you need to break through the aloneness of grief, crisis, or overwhelming pressure, you remind yourself that you do not have to keep a stiff upper lip or hold yourself together because that is the "right" thing to do. Harold Kushner puts it well in *When Bad Things Happen to Good People*: ". . . we can recognize that our anger at life's unfairness, our instinctive compassion at seeing people suffer, as coming from God, who teaches us to be angry at injustice and to feel compassion for the afflicted. Instead of feeling that we are opposed to God, we can feel that our indignation is God's anger at unfairness working through us, that when we cry out, we are still on God's side, and [God] . . . is still on ours."[6]

Embracing the Gift of Job's Wife

If you have ever traveled by car or plane, you have surely already (perhaps inadvertently) practiced the ritual of Job's wife. You are driving in heavy traffic on a hot summer day, and some idiot cuts you off. Or you're at the airport, on your way to your best friend's wedding in Atlanta. You have been waiting six hours for a flight that has been delayed and then cancelled due to what they are calling "mechanical difficulties" and then, when you are finally on another flight and you've taken off, the pilot announces, "Ladies and gentlemen, due to a 'weather-related situation' we are being rerouted to Pittsburgh."

Far be it from me to take God's name in vain or to use foul language in print, but the way most people respond to jerks on the road and to entirely messed up travel plans is by muttering (or shouting) some less refined version of "Gosh darn it," "For Pete's sake," "Jeepers," "Geewhiz," or "Holy moley."

Job's wife asks us—as a ritual practice—to notice each time we use such expressions. Not because she wants to censor us. *Au contraire.* She wants us to know that if we can curse when our defenses are down, then we can also recognize that when we choose to, we can tell God we have a bone to pick.

Like those hotels that leave a survey on your bed (along with two mint chocolates) on your last night, and ask, "Please fill out this questionnaire so that we can better serve you next time," Job's wife tells us to give God a report of what's going on down here—even—or especially—if it's bad news. At the very least, we may feel that we have not been abandoned.

CHAPTER 15

VASHTI
TAKING CARE OF YOURSELF

The Biblical Story

For one hundred and eighty days, Ahasuerus, King of Shushan, displayed the vast riches of his kingdom and the splendor of his majesty for all the men of Shushan to behold. At the end of this period, he held a banquet in the court of his palace garden. Royal wine in ornate golden beakers was served in abundance, as befits a king. The palace stewards were ordered to keep the wine flowing. "There will be no limits!" the king declared.

At the very same time, Queen Vashti, the wife of King Ahasuerus, held her own splendid banquet elsewhere in the palace for the women.

On the seventh day of the king's feasting and drinking, when the king was utterly drunk, King Ahasuerus ordered his seven eunuchs to bring Queen Vashti before him wearing her royal crown so he could display her beauty to the people and the officials. For she was a beautiful woman.

But Queen Vashti refused to come at the king's command.

The king burned with fury. He consulted his sages learned in procedures and asked them, "What shall be done, according to law, to Queen Vashti for failing to obey my command?" They advised him, "If it please Your Majesty, issue a royal edict that Vashti shall never enter the presence of King Ahasuerus." In this way, other women would be cautioned to obey their husbands.

—Adapted from Book of Esther 1

Vashti's Own Story

The women celebrating at Queen Vashti's women's banquet gave no thought to what the men were doing at the king's banquet. Their own banquet, seven days and going strong, was too compelling for them to care. It was easy enough to imagine how the men were partying: wine, stupidity, and grossness; made-up stories about lying with this woman, her sister, and her mother; throwing up and pissing contests. Grown men, all puffed up with themselves, acting like teenage boys left alone for the first time.

What fun the women had together, staying up so very late and sleeping on cushioned couches, piled high with pillows. Women of the most modest means pinched themselves: it was like a dream. Had they ever seen couches of gold and silver, room after room of alabaster, mother-of-pearl, and glimmering mosaic tiles? Even the wealthiest women were astonished by the delicacies being served: tiny vegetables filled with pine nuts, raisins, and cardamom. Only angels with the tiniest fingers could have carved and prepared them.

With so many wonderful parts of the women's banquet, who could say which was the best of all? There was dressing up together—not to impress, but to wrap each other in the many bolts of colored silks Queen Vashti had provided, and to pin them here and there with the jeweled clasps left in wicker baskets like golden grapes drying in the sun. "Turn around, dear. Look how the turquoise silk accents your bosom—no, no, no, wind it under your shoulder—how magnificent!" There were the hours to talk and talk—first getting the gossip out of the way, then weaving stories that seemed never to end, some so wonderfully sad they cried into each other's sleeves.

And dancing. Women danced in circles with cymbals and ribbons in their fingers; women snaked about in long lines, swerving around columns, going under one another's arms until they were all tangled into a tight knot. It was about the delight of moving, giving their bodies over to the rhythms of the horn players and drummers, being lost, but lost together, lost by choice.

It felt so safe.

Then, as if there had been an eclipse of the sun that no one expected, and day suddenly turned into night, the king's seven eunuchs stood timidly in the door of the women's banquet. They knew their entrance would break the spell, the enchantment and intense privacy of women celebrating together.

The chief of the eunuchs told his story, apologetically almost, hardly siding with the king who had ordered the eunuchs into the women's chambers.

"It happened just like this: One drunken guest of the king boasted, 'The women of Media are more beautiful.' Another, staggering, countered, 'The Persian women are even more beautiful.' The king was, by my reckoning, by far the most drunk of all, and, with Her Majesty's forgiveness, I repeat his very words: 'The one I screw is no Median; she's no Persian. She's a Chaldean. You have never seen anyone more beautiful in your lives. You want to see for yourselves?' The king commands Queen Vashti to come and dance before the men."

The Vashti in their midst was an enchanted mother, the one whose generosity, whose delight in her own womanhood, enabled the other women to discover what magic had been theirs all along. With her here among them, they felt whole. The younger women fretted for themselves, fearing that without Vashti, their own celebration would be over. But the older women despaired for Vashti, for they knew how such stories ended: Vashti, taken to the King's banquet, would be made into a dancing monkey.

And so much worse—horrible, horrible, they knew. The king would command the eunuchs to strip her of her robes. Vashti would beg the king, "Let me at least keep on my undergarment, like a harlot." And the men would jeer, "Strip her, strip her naked." Vashti would beg the king, "If your men find me beautiful, they will take me for themselves and they will kill you. If they find me plain, they'll disgrace you. All you are is a stable boy who surrounds himself with cheap harlots; you may sit on the throne, but you are trash."

Vashti would be made to stand naked, except for the crown on her head. With every man staring, the king would rub himself against her, making her play the captive maiden. And then he would clap his hands and command: "Dance for me, Vashti. Dance for me and show us what you've got." This is what would happen to Vashti, the women's queen, and afterward, when they brought her back to her chambers, she would never be the same.

Then Vashti did the impossible, and she did it as though she had been planning it her whole life. She refused to go before the king.

"I will not go," she told the eunuchs, matter-of-factly. They just stood there, stunned, her words failing to register. "Tell him I refuse." No anger in her voice, just resolve. No, she would not do it. Not this time, not ever.

The women saw Vashti taking care of herself by saying "no." They knew she was taking care of them too, by modeling what they often imagined doing themselves, but too rarely did. She showed that the boundaries of a woman's dignity may not be violated. She demonstrated that any woman, not just a queen, could say: "Not now, not unless it's on my terms as well, not unless I'm fully comfortable, not unless I am treated with dignity." Only a woman who is respected can be expected to show respect.

"I will not go." Her words stayed in the women's heads in the days after they had left the banquet, as they brushed their daughters' hair. They could say it too, and they could teach it to their daughters. They practiced the words in their heads: "I will not go."

The women worried what would happen to Vashti now, but they needn't have. As her "punishment" for not appearing before her husband, the foolish king forbade her from coming before him! A comedy, truly. "What an idiot," Vashti laughed. "He thinks he is punishing me? He has given me the gift I have always wanted: my dignity!"

The women laughed too, as they heard the king's advisors go from town to town proclaiming the king's royal edict: "No woman may disrespect her husband."

Vashti Speaks to Us

Queen Vashti is less well known than Queen Esther, the beautiful and demure Jewish woman who replaced her, who hid her identity from the king, and then, encouraged by her Uncle Mordechai, saved the Jews when they were threatened with annihilation. Young girls may have heard the story of the two queens as a morality tale: If you are like Vashti, independent, assertive, and confrontational, and disobey the people who tell you what to do, you will get kicked out of the palace.

Be like Esther instead. Be pretty enough to win a beauty contest, be compliant, and you'll save your people and wear pretty queen's robes as you live happily ever after.

Feminism has reread the Book of Esther. And while Queen Esther has not been demoted as a role model, Queen Vashti has been plucked from the gutter and reclaimed as a heroine. And well she should be: she is not the loser who gets kicked out of the palace (many assume she was killed, but there is no evidence of that)—she is the winner, who generously shares her reward with us.

This is the gift of Vashti. She empowers us to take care of ourselves. She teaches us to rehearse the words "I will not go," and to use them whenever the boundaries we define for ourselves are threatened by any man or woman. Vashti teaches that when we refuse to enter unsafe spaces, we are taking good care of ourselves. Vashti demonstrates that we have the right and duty to ourselves to set limits for others.

Unlike the more docile and politic Queen Esther, Vashti does not worry about being a nice girl (although Queen Esther may not be as nice as she seems, for she exploits her "nice girl" façade in the service of heavy-duty politicking). Vashti does not swallow indignities and no one will make her feel cheap. Vashti makes waves when she needs to and is willing to disturb the status quo. Plain and simple, she will not be violated. You do not mess with Vashti and you do not cross her. She is, as Jewish feminist Mary Gendler once called her, "the role model for appropriate self-assertion."

The story of Queen Vashti refusing to dance naked before the king and all the men is, most evidently, a story about a woman who refuses to have her personal and physical boundaries violated. We read about the violation of women's boundaries all the time in newspapers, in one version or another, and it makes us furious. The consequences of abuse, particularly for younger women, are especially severe, according to a study appearing in the August 2001 edition of the *Journal of the American Medical Association*. This study discovered that 20 percent of adolescent girls who date are victimized by physical and sexual violence: hitting, slapping, being shoved, or being forced to have sex.

But it doesn't stop there. Later, girls are more likely to experience serious health problems, including drug abuse, binge drinking, eating disorders, risky sexual behaviors such as unprotected intercourse, teenage pregnancy, and suicide attempts. These figures are troubling, and it gets worse for adult women: 25 percent experience violence when dating. Both younger and older women are highly vulnerable to depression when they have been abused and degraded.[1] But we knew this already: when a woman believes she is too vulnerable to protect herself from violence, she suffers.

Vashti's story is not only about our right to protect the boundaries of our bodies from violence and abuse. We have the right to protect our personal boundaries in our homes. Like Virginia Woolf, we have the right to claim a room of our own; we have the right to say, "I need a day away to get recharged" or, more simply, to say, "Not right now."

Vashti's story is also about protecting the boundaries of our physical space—our desks, our mail, our homes. Vashti tells us that when our families come to visit, they cannot rearrange our living rooms or give our clothing to charity without asking because they think they are doing us a favor. It's about protecting our time: schools should not schedule performances and programs to which parents are invited in the middle of the work day, as if we were all, or ought to be, stay-at-home parents.

Vashti's message is also about protecting our intellectual space: people cannot use our ideas without crediting us or thanking us for them. And it's about protecting our professional space: people may not sexually harass us, explicitly or through innuendo, even when they think their attentions are really flattering us. People may not pay us less money or respect us less for doing the same job as men.

This powerful message continues to show us how to protect our psychic space. The people we live with are not permitted to try to read our minds and decide we wouldn't mind it if they invited company for dinner on Friday. They cannot tell us, "I know you don't really like the present I gave you," and they cannot tell us, "You think you have a stomach virus, but I know your symptoms are really emotional." When we have good and healthy fights with our partners, they cannot tell us that the issue at hand is our problem, or that we should get our heads examined, or that if we weren't premenstrual or going through menopause, we wouldn't be getting so worked up. No, says Vashti, I refuse to let you treat me that way.

Once, at work, I had a full-blown Vashti experience. I discovered that I had been set up as the fall guy to shift the blame away from people higher up in the organization who were actually responsible for a substantial bungle. I was asked to go along and take the blame because it was "for the good of the organization." Oh, right. I was ready to scream, stomp away, and quit, but a wise colleague, a woman executive who had fought her share of battles, advised me to take what I can only call "the Vashti route."

Catching me just before I exploded, my colleague pulled me into her office, shut the door, and said, "I know you are angry, and you have every reason in the world to be. But are you sure you really want to walk away right now and burn all your bridges behind you?" I was indeed angry enough to want to quit, but, I realized, why should I be the one to lose my salary and have to look for a new job? I didn't really want to leave: it was a prestigious institution, I did important work, and I worked with some terrific people.

My colleague advised: "If you want to stay, you have to call the shots and set the terms so you feel safe and protected." She gave me ideas about how I could take the Vashti route. One idea was to write down what I thought needed to be changed in order for me to stay, and to present my plan as an ultimatum. The next day, my voice quivering and my knees shaking (I had gotten the substance but not the style of Vashti's regal refusal), I went before the boss. I began: "You may not treat me as the fall guy. Not now, not ever again." I then carefully presented what I believed I contributed to the organization, and I described how I, and other employees, could and should be treated with more respect.

I was able to successfully convince my boss to institute some better policies. I learned that women who act in the spirit of Vashti, refusing to have their boundaries violated, can sometimes successfully communicate with those who threaten to violate them. They make the reason for their anger clear and they express it in no uncertain terms. They demand that their violators back off and catch themselves in the future, so that there is no next time. Women acting in the spirit of Vashti can succeed in educating those who would step over boundaries, and in doing so, they make the world a safer place for themselves and others.

Other times, when a woman acts in the spirit of Vashti, saying, "You can't do this to me," instead of hearing apologies and promises to get it right next time, she gets kicked out by the King Ahasuerus in her life:

her boss fires her, her boyfriend doesn't call for another date, her mother threatens, "Well if you can't appreciate the way I rearranged your cupboards, then you won't find me doing it ever again." This scenario, harsh at first, is sometimes the better one for the long term, because it allows you to stop holding on to illusions that things will get better. And there's a consolation: you know you will not be violated by this person again. True, you may pay other real prices—after all, Vashti no longer had accommodations in the palace—but you will not be humiliated. You will find new and safe spaces—literal and psychic ones—and you will enter into mutually respectful relationships.

I am not suggesting that it is easy to be assertive. Being assertive is a skill few women are trained in; it's a capacity we may have been trained to forget we have. More likely, we've been taught to suppress our own needs and be compliant. We may be so good at suppressing our own feelings that in effect, we hardly feel at all. When we would rightfully seethe with rage, we go emotionally flat.

I am not suggesting either that we can always be as assertive as Vashti. Sometimes we choose to keep quiet about a certain offense because we have a different, bigger battle to fight. Sometimes we have no choice but to work with impossible people until we can find a new way to make a living.

One is not born knowing how to act in Vashti mode, just as one isn't born knowing how to play piano, ski, or perform heart surgery. Anything truly worth knowing requires learning and practice. Refusing to be humiliated is our right: knowing how to do it is a skill we can cultivate and practice.

Embracing the Gift of Vashti

To act in the spirit of Vashti, you will need a crown to remind you and announce to others that you have the right to do what is necessary to preserve your dignity. True, you might not actually go out wearing your crown, unless you were born into a royal family (even then, you'd probably only retrieve it from cold storage for state occasions). But you do need to own a crown, and place it somewhere you and others can see it easily, to remind you of your right to define your own boundaries.

When I joined the department in which I now teach, I noticed that almost every woman colleague had a silver crown from a novelty store placed on a shelf in her office. I didn't ask anyone about the crowns for a while; I just observed. I thought it might have something to do with women protecting themselves, but I didn't want to presume. Then one day, one of the women, who had successfully emerged from a trying professional battle, presented me with my own crown, studded with plastic emeralds and rubies. All she said was, "Now you have one of your own if you ever need it," and I knew that it was the crown of Vashti. When other women join our ranks, we make sure they have crowns of Vashti too (I confess, I'm crazy about all kinds of sparkling accessories, so I've been distributing magic wands to my women colleagues at our annual end-of-the-year picnic). Get yourself a glorious crown, or make one, and give one to a woman or girl you care about enough to help her preserve her dignity.

You may not be the crown type—you may need to acquire a more practical piece of equipment, or one you can use every day or even take with you that symbolizes the power of your boundaries. I recently purchased items to meet both needs: a fabulous ergonomic chair for my home office that goes up and down and spins (unlike the old kitchen chair I used to use) and a very sophisticated, classy briefcase (to replace the backpack I've been using ever since my daughter passed it down to me when she graduated from high school, saying it was too dorky for her). It's only been a few days, but sitting in the chair or holding the briefcase, I feel unusually safe.

PART VI

BEING IN THE DIVINE PRESENCE

CHAPTER 16

LEAH
FEELING BLESSED

The Biblical Story

God saw that Leah was not loved. Leah's husband, Jacob, loved his other wife, her sister Rachel, far more than he loved her. As a consolation and as a comfort, God made it easy for Leah to give birth, opening her womb. God had done this before for Hagar, causing her to give birth to a son as a sign that a good woman's suffering was noticed. A child: a token of God's love.

One after another, Leah had three sons. Like Adam, she took the power to name each new creature as it came into being, and in each name, she discovered the name for her desires.

When her first baby was born, Leah named him Reuben, the son of seeing. For Leah, his name meant, "God has seen my affliction, and now my husband will love me." Though God evidently saw her pain, Leah saw that Jacob did not grow to love her more. She saw this all too plainly: bearing his child did not make a difference.

Time passed, and Leah conceived and gave birth once again. She named her second baby Simeon, the son of hearing. For Leah, his name meant, "God has heard that I was not loved," and this was true, for God had indeed heard. Simeon was the clear sign of that. But Leah heard no evidence that Jacob loved her more.

Again time passed; again Leah gave birth. She named her third baby Levi, the son who joins my husband to me. This name was a hope, a prayer. To her it meant, "This time, my husband will finally become attached to me, because I have given him three sons." Her arms were filled with three wonderful boys, signs of God's attachment and continued involvement in her life. How profoundly she was blessed with children. But still her husband did not grow closer to her.

Leah and Jacob continued to make love. Leah became pregnant, giving birth this time to a fourth son. Fours sons! By now, Leah knew it was foolhardy to go on hoping that any number of children could ever make Jacob love her more. But there was no denying it: this child was yet another sign that God was there to see, hear, and come close to her. So Leah exclaimed, "This time, I will thank the Lord!" Which is why she named him Judah, for it meant just this. She praised God because she was thankful for the abundant blessing, these four children, that she had received.

—Adapted from Genesis 29:31–35

Leah's Own Story

Leah is gathering figs for the evening meal, reaching over her pregnant belly, grown so wonderfully big. She is cautious not to reach up for the figs on the higher branches—the grandmothers have prohibited her from stretching upward, lest the baby inside her become entangled. Leah recalls how she has noticed every single glorious change in her body since the baby inside her began to grow. The day she knew her blood didn't flow. The day her breasts began to puff and then swell. The stretching out of her belly. Even the little knob her belly button started to make. What wonders her body can perform, making a life, and so effortlessly.

They say she is weak-eyed, but Leah misses nothing. She scrutinizes Jacob's attitude toward her, thinking she might detect a shift in his feelings about her. He is always polite, solicitous of her well-being. He stares at her large stomach as she cuts the figs, and she sees him pull in his breath so that his shoulders rise up. He will be so very proud of himself to become a father; already he holds himself with a new weightiness. Rachel is kneading dough beside her, and Leah watches Jacob's eyes move from her own large belly to the strands of hair that have fallen over Rachel's eyes. She sees him caress Rachel's cheek.

Leah pictures herself with her baby in her arms; she pictures herself handing the child to Jacob. She imagines what it might be like if Jacob, so filled with child love, might lean over their baby and stroke her cheek as well.

Years later, when Leah carries her fourth child in her womb, figs are not yet in season, and so she makes a preserve of sweet lemons and almonds. She is no less awed by the brilliance of her body to make life. She still imagines that Jacob, by now a tender friend, will hunger for her, place his hand at the small of her back, and pull her toward him. But now it is a thought that passes, no longer a dream. She shifts her own gaze to her boys, the delicious boys, and thinks, "I can praise God for what I do have or rail at God for what I have not." She wraps her arms around Levi, a toddler already, who can't decide if he wants to stay in his mother's arms or squirm away. "I praise God with all my soul," Leah says in her heart as Levi taps at her belly, asking, "Is anybody in there?" "I am blessed," Leah decides, and suddenly she is clear about what she will name her new baby, if he should be born in good health. "He will be Judah, my child who will always turn me toward God in thanks."

Leah Speaks to Us

Leah has every reason to feel spiritually empty and abandoned by God. Her father, Laban, who considered himself saddled with this unmarried older daughter, tricks Jacob into taking her as his first wife, when her sister Rachel is the one Jacob has loved and labored for. Jacob does not love Leah, and Leah grows painfully jealous of her sister. On top of parent trouble, husband trouble, and sister trouble, Leah at first also has fertility trouble. When Leah does finally give birth after a spell of barrenness, she hopes that at least her husband troubles will be over. But her babies do nothing to win Jacob's love. In response, Leah could have chosen bitterness as her stance toward life. She could have chosen to curse God. Instead, she chooses to bless God for all the love she has been given. Leah, the so-called unloved one, chooses to experience herself as the beloved of God.

Leah has a spiritual gift, the ability to name each and every thing for which she is grateful. She doesn't feel happiness as a vague wish. She notices all the particulars, and she puts her gratitude into words: "I thank you, God, for the miracle of seeing my baby's chest move up and down as he breathes. I thank you, God, for the milk that is spurting so quickly from my breasts." Leah's spiritual gift is a form of prayer, a streaming conversation that takes place sometimes silently, in her head, overheard by no one. But more often, she will give voice to her delight. Praising God for her sons, for her sister, for Jacob, for the sheep on the grassy hills, for the almond flowers, she feels connected to every other human being, as if she were tied by strands of gratitude to everything and everyone in creation.

For Leah, naming is a rigorous spiritual discipline. She tells herself at each moment, "Name the beauty you are witnessing, name the aroma you smell. Don't let a detail escape you." For Leah, naming a child is best of all, because each name is a prayer, one she can repeat each time she calls her child: "Simeon, where are you?" "Hush, Judah, don't cry. Mamma is here." Saying each name awakens her to God's close presence. Saying each name, Leah witnesses: God is not so far away, but is attached to her and to her children; God will love her and God will see her, even if Jacob cannot.

Leah does not go about blessing God as many men have done. She pens no psalms. She erects no stone altars. She sacrifices no animals. Her experience of God does not take place in an official building or under the direct supervision of clergy. Leah is like the many religious women who approach God quite autonomously, engaging in rituals that dramatize social ties with God, ancestors, family, and community. Leah's style of blessing is immediate, personal, and informal. She blesses by naming.

If you've been to a baby-naming or baby-welcoming ceremony, you know how moving it is to hear the story of how the new baby got its name. Surrounded by family and friends, the new parents cradle their baby in all four of their arms. They talk through tears, speaking words that come from their hearts, and not from bound prayer books or photocopied sheets someone handed them. "We are naming our child David, in honor of his great-grandmother Dora, who always had a kind word for everyone she met. We hope that David will emulate Dora in this way. His middle name is Charles, after Grandpa Charlie, who was known for his modesty, his sense of humor, and his deep love of family." In the names we choose for our children, we reach into our histories, bringing back glimmers of the souls of the people we've lost and need to have back with us. We also move forward, jump-starting our children's personalities, hoping they will be defined by the worthy traits of their namesakes. We do not need ritual experts to tell us which name to choose, nor do we need official texts to tell us how to narrate the story of our child's name. We know that the souls of Dora and Charles won't replicate themselves in David Charles without our effort. We learn how to elicit and sustain those souls in our child.

One ancient midrash about the meanings of the names Leah chooses for the first four sons she and Jacob have comes from the tractate, or treatise, on blessings in the Babylonian Talmud. This tractate tells us how to be the kind of person who knows how to bless, and how to live ever attentive to blessings all around. This particular story was passed on from one rabbi to another, and it is a story we continue to tell today when we try to understand how feeling grateful connects to expressing gratitude. Not surprisingly, the model for someone who feels and expresses gratitude is Leah.

Since the creation of the world, no person offered thanks to the Blessed Holy One until Leah came along and thanked God. She said these very words: "This time, let me thank God," and she gave her fourth child the name Judah, meaning, "I will praise God."

Surely others before Leah thanked God. Didn't Noah, Abraham, and Jacob, who built altars to God as signs of thanksgiving, exclaim: "Thank you, God!" for their safety, or for the blessings they were promised, or for the child they were given? But they did not demonstrate their gratitude in the same way.

Leah, according to midrash, was the first to transform her feelings of gratitude into language, creating the words of prayer. Believing that she had received more than her rightful share of goodness and blessing, believing she had gotten more than she deserved, she created a new way of being in the world. She praised God with the language of prayer for the abundance of her good fortune. Not only does Leah create a simple, straightforward language of prayer to thank God for receiving more than she ever expected, but she also becomes known as a person who both experiences and expresses her gratitude.

Leah is telling us that when we feel more grateful than we could ever anticipate, we should stop to give words to our feelings. Name them. Name all the goodness we have received. And then go one step further. Dare to let others overhear the voice in our heart that says, "I can't believe this good thing that has happened to me! It is a blessing from God." We must allow ourselves to be known as someone who is mesmerized by what we do have, someone who can tell God directly, "I thank you for what you have done for me."

Leah's model of blessing God works like this for me: When I am fully awake to wonder and my whole being is awash in prayerfulness, I hear a mantra in my head, not three times or one hundred times, but the entire day. "Thank you, thank you, thank you, thank you, thank you" it goes when I am in "general gladness" mode. When I am in "specific gladness" mode, it can go: "Thank you for my cat's furry white stomach, for the cruet of raspberry vinegar in my pantry, for *Gaudy Night* by Dorothy Sayers, for the wedding part of the 'Sunday Style' section of the *New York Times*, for Sudafed Sinus tablets, for Julie baking biscotti with Grandma Ruth, for Helena's mother recovering from her heart attack, for my student Elizabeth sending an e-mail from Honduras to say she arrived safely."

I imagine this is how Leah worshipped God, by letting her gratitude well up and by silently saying "thank you," then naming the reason she blesses. It's worship as a way of being, worship as a way of engaging God and everyday life at the same time. In her every action—playing with her children, baking, gardening, sleeping well, and making love— Leah is praying, praying with her whole being.

I witnessed new, but already dear, friends of mine, a young married couple, engaging in Leah-like worship on a Sabbath eve. In lieu of singing his wife's praises with the traditional words of the "Woman of Valor" proverb, the husband chanted, "In the *spirit* of the proverb, I praise you for being such a kind soul; I praise you for filling our home with beautiful flowers and supporting us all materially and emotionally." His wife, in turn, chanted to him, "In the spirit of the proverb, I praise you for all the work you have done strengthening the foundation of our home (she meant this literally—he had been pouring cement all week); I praise you for having decided to become a Literacy Volunteer; I praise you for really being there when your cousin was in crisis and needed to hear your voice; I praise you for the humor you bring to our lives." It was one of the most exquisite ceremonies I had ever witnessed. They were not just speaking words of praise to each other; they were praising God too, saying, "Thank you for all this."

Unlike Leah and this young couple, who publicize their gratitude, some hesitate to let others know the particulars of their grace. Some feel safer keeping the contents of their gratitude private. When you make your thankfulness public, you show all your cards, revealing what matters to you most of all. When you allow others to overhear you naming your heart's desire and the pleasures that stun you, they will come to know you intimately.

By naming, Leah lets the world know she is radiantly blessed. You may hesitate to make your gratitude public fearing not just the intimacy, but also that you will tempt fate. I know this one well: A friend asks, "How is everything?" I take stock of my situation, and every so often, I can conclude, "Oh my God! Everything is unbelievably perfect. Health. Family. Love. Work. Peace in my little corner of the world." I want to say it all, to name every single perfect thing in the landscape of my life, from the success of one daughter's enormous surgery to the miracle of the other daughter's actually finding a pair of sandals she liked. But I am halted, even if I am certain the details of my good fortune will not bore my listener who truly wishes me well. A creepy voice of doom warns: "Name even one piece of your happiness and you jeopardize it all." Swallowing my delight, I summarize: "Everything is fine, thanks. And how are you?" Earlier generations explained that mentioning your good fortune was a form of boasting, which ignited the jealousy of others. Their jealousy translated into the "evil eye," a malicious spirit that threatens all precious blessings.

Leah rejoices because she gets more than she believes she deserves. How do we know what we deserve in life? How can we know when we have gotten less than we deserve or when we have gotten more than our due? It's curious that we measure our joys and sorrows with the word *deserve*, as if there were a relationship between what human beings, in general, ought to experience in life and what we, in particular, because of who we are and what we have done, deserve. But we say that all the time: "She deserves a good husband"; "After what he went through, he deserves a little bit of happiness." You would think we were prophets, intuiting what our personal outcome ought to be, then feeling sad or glad, depending on how well or how poorly we measured up.

We receive our lives; we do not deserve them. Leah is able to praise God abundantly for what she has received, even when her heart holds pain. But Leah can tease away the good from the bad, and the bad doesn't obscure or diminish the good. She can celebrate that well-filled portion of her cup and, without deluding herself, be sustained by it.

This breeze in the thickly hot part of summer, this slice of cheese—old, but still fresh—this summer morning when almost everything has gone wrong until a friend calls to say, "I was just thinking of you," this teenage child who looks at your outfit and judges, "You actually look good." A Leah blessing is so simple, so pure, so true. You need only name it.

Embracing the Gift of Leah

You can easily bless as Leah does. You take all the goodness you are aware of and you put it into words, giving it a name. When you feel blessed by others, tell them in their presence or in a letter specifically how they are a blessing to you. My mother (whose name also happens to be Leah) often taught me, "If you have something good to say to a person, let them know. Don't assume they know it in their own hearts, even if it's someone you think is so important and so confident that he or she doesn't need praise." I have taken her advice and put it into action hundreds of times. People tell me that it is the best gift they have received, kind words that tell them precisely how they are appreciated. Don't worry if your expression of gratitude is long overdue—it is never too late to express it.

Here's an example of a Leah-like blessing by a woman I know, also coincidentally named Leah, who gave this toast of blessing to her mother at a sixty-fifth birthday celebration:

This milestone birthday gives me a great opportunity to celebrate all the wonderful qualities my mother possesses. Like my namesake, Leah, I know we shouldn't be afraid to name our blessings out loud and to be thankful for them.

Well, I'm thankful for my mother. I'm thankful for how she listens to me and laughs harder at my jokes than anyone else. I'm thankful for her love and for her playful spirit. I'm thankful for how beautiful she always looks. I'm thankful that the last time we played tennis she got annoyed when I won a few points. I'm thankful for having a mother I can tease and whom I can scold when she doesn't drink enough water or go to bed on time, or other minor infractions.

When people ask me how my mother is, I tell them what a great time this is in her life, how she is floating on a cloud about being a grandparent. How she is healthy and strong. How she is about to embark on a new business venture. I'm incredibly thankful for all these blessings and for my mother's happiness.

Use this toast as an example, and think of blessings for which you are grateful. Then take the next opportunity to express your gratitude.

CHAPTER 17

HANNAH
SEEKING GOD

The Biblical Story

Elkanah had two wives, one named Hannah and the other Peninah. Peninah had children, but Hannah was childless. Elkanah used to go up from his town every year to worship and offer sacrifices to the Lord at Shiloh. One day, Elkanah offered a sacrifice. He used to give a portion to Peninah for all her sons and daughters, but to Hannah he would give a full portion, for Hannah was his favorite. . . .

The Lord had closed Hannah's womb. To make her miserable, her rival would taunt her that the Lord had made her childless. This happened year after year. Every time Hannah ascended to the House of the Lord, Peninah taunted her, so that she wept and would not eat. Elkanah said to her, "Hannah, why do you cry and why don't you eat? Am I not better than ten sons?"

After they had eaten and drunk at Shiloh, Hannah rose. Eli the priest was sitting near the doorpost of the temple. Feeling the bitterness of her soul, Hannah prayed to the Lord, weeping all the while. She vowed: "O Lord of Hosts, if you will look upon the suffering of your servant and remember me and not forget me, and if you grant me a son, I will devote him to God all the days of his life, and no razor shall ever touch his head." As she prayed, Eli observed her mouth. Hannah was praying in her heart. As only her lips moved and her voice could not be heard, Eli thought she was drunk. "You are making a drunken spectacle of yourself," he said. "Sober up!" Hannah replied, "Oh no, I am a woman of deep sorrow. I am not drunk. I am pouring out my soul to God. I am not worthless: all this time, I have been speaking out of my anguish and distress." "Go in peace," said Eli, "and may the God of Israel give you what you have asked for." She answered, "You are most kind." She left and she ate and was no longer depressed. Early the next morning, they worshipped God and returned home to Ramah.

Elkanah knew his wife Hannah, and the Lord remembered her. Hannah conceived and at the turn of the year, bore a son. She named him Samuel, meaning, "I asked the Lord for him."

When she had weaned him, she took him to the House of the Lord at Shiloh and brought him to Eli the priest. She said, "I am the woman who stood here beside you and prayed to God. It is this child I prayed for, and the Lord has granted me what I asked. I, in turn, lend him to God for as long as he lives."

. . . Samuel was engaged in the service of the Lord as an attendant. His mother made a little robe for him and brought it to him each year when she made the pilgrimage with her husband to make the annual sacrifice. Eli blessed Elkanah and his wife, saying, "May God grant you children by this woman in place of the loan she has made to God." The Lord took note of Hannah: she conceived and bore three sons and two daughters.

—Adapted from I Samuel 1–2

Hannah's Own Story

"You shouldn't count on my helping to prepare for Shiloh this year," Peninah told Hannah.

The Day of Atonement was coming to a close, the sun sinking below the hills, the sepia sky becoming dark. The pilgrimage festival of Sukkoth tumbled toward them in just four days, and with it came endless preparation.

"I'm sorry it all falls on you," Peninah rattled on. "I don't have to tell you I have my hands filled nursing the newborn and keeping my eye on all the others. What would we do without you, Hannah? If you had children of your own, you'd never be as devoted an aunt. So this really is for the best, a gift for us all. I should be the jealous one, you know. You have the better deal: all my children to love without the agony of labor. And so much more of Elkanah."

"Obviously you're busy," Hannah said, slicing bread they would soon dip into yogurt to end the fast. Peninah could turn any conversation into an opportunity to push Hannah's childlessness in her face. It stopped mattering: Peninah's words no longer wounded her. Even if the mood of forgiveness of the holy days hadn't been so central in her mind, Hannah would have still pardoned Peninah for the clumsiness of her words.

What would they need to pack to bring to Shiloh? The thought of the whole enterprise energized Hannah, even when she should have been weak from the day of solemn fasting. This year in Shiloh she would speak to God in her own voice.

Before dawn, before anyone else stirred, Hannah worked methodically, packing food baskets with dried fruits and flat breads she had been preparing during the Days of Awe, filling water jugs and piling bedding onto the donkeys. Hannah could narrate each journey to Shiloh, so dependably the same.

Her whole life she had been making this trip to the sanctuary in Shiloh to offer sacrifices, first as a child with her parents and now with her husband, Elkanah; his second wife, Peninah; and Peninah's children. They took bulls, rams, perfect yearling lambs, the meal offering of fine flour and oil, the drink offering of undiluted wine, the ripest first fruits they had set aside, guarded and polished. Once they reached the main road from the hills of Ephraim to Shiloh, they would weave themselves into the caravan of other pilgrim families ribboning their way upward. Elkanah would lead the way, as Hannah's father had done. The ordering of their parade gave the illusion that the men had choreographed the entire enterprise and not just gathered in the bulls and rams at the last minute with much fanfare and the barking of orders.

Going to Shiloh, the families packed the heaviness in their hearts and the weight of their guilt and imperfection. If they were so graced, they packed the overflowing basket of their joy and brought it before God. Once in Shiloh, after the priests sacrificed the offerings and returned leftover portions of this and that, there was a place for all that feeling. If the people attended these pilgrimages as a family, they were made holy together and it brought them closer, not just to God, but to each other. That's what people said. Would this were so, Hannah wished. Since childhood, she had quietly been doubting the efficacy of the ceremony of sacrifice, wondering if it was indeed God's will.

At first, Hannah had not been jealous of Peninah. She was happy for her, happy to hold a fretful, sleepless baby over her knees so Peninah could get a little rest. She was confident her time would come. After each lovemaking, she pressed her hand on her stomach to feel her child erupting into life, to mark the moment of God's blessing.

She felt nothing.

Months of waiting, then years. When you wait too long for a blessing you expect, it starts to feel as if you have disappeared in God's eye. Hannah inventoried her life like a merchant. God did not punish for a good heart and good works. It must be an oversight. God, the accountable one, would catch the error. She waited, not for a miracle but for a correction.

Preparing for Shiloh this year, once again, Hannah had no basket of joy to bring before God, only her emptiness and the wish to engage God.

These past months, unfamiliar waves of darkness had settled on Hannah, threatening her resolve to remain confident in the future. First she cried easily without provocation. Over nothing really: a donkey refused to come at her call, a cup of goat's milk she had prepared for Peninah's toddler had spilled. Some mornings, her body felt too heavy to rise up from her bedding, and she forgot to eat unless she was reminded. Retreating into her tent for hours, the only thing that gave her peace was the thought that in Shiloh, God might hear her voice, offered in a new way.

Before embarking for Shiloh, Elkanah beckoned to Hannah. "Come stand with me under the pomegranate trees." He tempted her with the bruised red seeds he unpacked hastily from their chalky white casing. "You have me. I love you best. What else do you need?"

She had tried many times to explain. All his love and his constant appetite for her could not make Hannah whole. She wished it could.

As Hannah and the entire entourage of their family took their last steps as they approached Shiloh for the Sukkoth festival, the whole enterprise of sacrifice seemed more problematic to Hannah than ever before. Did the smell of burning flesh, however disguised with frankincense, move God to look down on the ones offering it and experience their gratitude? Was divine favor apt to be showered more abundantly on the wealthy families whose offerings were more dazzling? Did burning pigeons animate God to see into a person's heart and feel where the hurting was? The foods, the fires, the chanting priests with their showy arm-waving and croaking chants, the retinue of serious but awkward and still pimply priests-in-training balancing gold and silver plates and jumping to fetch and cleanse the copper lavers and tongs. A generous, all-knowing God could not require this lavish and groveling display chock-full of rules and regulations. Who wears the fine linen robes, who carries the offering, who raises up his hands, who fans the flames, who eats the most excellent parts, and who eats the remains: were these the details that pleased the God of Abraham and Sarah?

To Hannah, their own sacrificial practices resembled the idolatries of the star worshippers, so heatedly disparaged by her people. The sacrificing was meant to satisfy people, not God. It was a concession God made to humans who failed to imagine how they might otherwise come into the divine presence and make their lives holy.

Surely the brighter priests or the tribal elders had to know this. Why didn't they let on? Out of habit? Out of respect for the old ways they had inherited from their ancestors?

Hannah and her family arrived at the temple by late morning. Hannah watched how Elkanah relished the liveliness of this year's sacrifice ceremonies. What great power he found in it. When the priest thrust his knife into the neck of the bleating animal, when the blood splashed and poured, Elkanah breathed out and his shoulders caved into his chest. Hannah could see the color fall from his face, then return to rosy redness as he experienced being cleansed of guilt. The violence soothed him like nothing else. He cried loudly; then, composing himself, he hugged Peninah's children as if they had just been brought back to life. He patted lonely looking supplicants on the back and pressed coins into the hands of anyone who remotely looked like a beggar. "And you, my love, the love of my heart." He embraced Hannah, saving her for last. "We feel so utterly filled up," he said, assuming the overflow of his euphoria.

Whatever her own misgivings about the bloody sacrifices, being a spectator to Elkanah's piety moved Hannah. Without intending disrespect, Hannah still wondered, what did this impressive engagement of Elkanah's senses and the jolting of his tendered emotions mean to God? Elkanah returned to the family, bringing portions of the roasted meat. Hannah held back, lurking in the shadows of the temple.

She would attempt to enter God's presence without the paraphernalia: no goats, no knives, no blood. Without intermediaries: no priests. Just the words in her heart. Just a sacrifice of deeds, the gift one made of one's own life that required no destruction, only an inventive generosity.

Hannah felt her darkness lifting, hurtling her forward with optimism. She knew she had to act with resolve lest she lose her courage. She moved up to the edge of the altar. Attendants were pouring bucketfuls of water on the stone grounds, readying the offering area for the next day. No one noticed Hannah, a countrywoman wrapped in scarves covered in the dust of the traveler.

With empty hands, without the priest's liturgical formula, Hannah came before God. Closing her eyes, she spoke from her heart, her lips moving and her voice silent:

Source of love, source of sorrow,
Source of light and darkness,
It is I, Hannah. I am calling to you and I need you to hear me.
I can cry no more.
See me before I disappear into the hole of my grief.
A man's love is not enough. Your love is not enough.
See the pain I hold and feel it with me, so I am not alone.
I pray for a child. I can feel the child in my arms, I can feel all
*   the love.*
Bless me with a child and I will thank you:
I will never forget the child is not mine, but your gift.
For my part
I will raise the child to embrace goodness,
To mark the holy,
To register wonder,

To take care.
Your presence will flow through this child.
This, I promise.

"Madam," said Eli the old priest, noticing her as he made his rounds. "Madam," he repeated, tapping Hannah on the shoulder. His presence shocked her and she gasped, bringing her out of her tearful trance. "What is this bizarre pantomime? What are you doing? This is a place of worship."

"I pray God will know that, too," said Hannah. She knew God had heard her prayer. She felt lightness as she went on her way. Glimmers of expectation rose, enough to sustain her. As she waited for her prayer to be answered, she began to imagine how she might make good on her promise, to raise a child bound to God. She would borrow wool from Peninah and she would start to weave sacred garments for her child.

Hannah Speaks to Us

Hannah teaches us to negotiate with God and ask for what we need. The ritual resources available to Hannah, who so badly wanted a child of her own, did not suit her spiritual sensibilities. In her culture, there were rituals aplenty for cleansing yourself from sin, for marking the pilgrimage holidays, for circumcising your newborn son. Most of the rituals involved the violence of fire or the cut of a knife, and some required the participation of ritual experts born into the priestly class. Expert in the rules and regulations, they were rewarded with status and honor. But there was no formal, public ritual for a woman struggling with unmet needs, in Hannah's case, the desire to bear children.

In our generation, women of many traditions have acknowledged that the spiritual means available to them have been either insufficient or inappropriate. Women now boldly make sacred all kinds of previously unmarked occurrences in a woman's biological life, such as menarche, menstruation, infertility, conception, pregnancy, labor, delivery, and menopause. We do so with new liturgies that are sensitive to the different ways women talk to God and about God. Most of the new women's rituals, even when developed by female religious leaders, can generally be performed without trained, ordained professionals officiating. Highly accessible, they are open to lay people who are free to improvise on the practices and personalize them to fit their lives.

Three thousand years ago, without the support of a feminist movement or the many bold and inventive female spiritual leaders we now have, Hannah became the first woman in the Bible who spoke her prayer to God in a public setting. Hannah's direct and intimate speech to God was such an unusual form of religious devotion for its time that Eli the priest, observing her, had no idea what she was doing. Who had ever stood in the temple, moving her lips and crying? Such odd behavior! It didn't conform to any way of worship that Eli recognized. Not imagining it could be a legitimate style of worship he didn't know about, Eli concluded Hannah had to be drunk! It is not surprising that a religious leader witnessing an unfamiliar expression of women's spirituality would decide that it was transgressive.

Scholar Leila Gal Berner sees the differences in worship styles in the story of Hannah as being gender-related: "Hannah speaks as a woman to God out of her own very personal anguish. She prays in an unstructured way, sharing her emotional state of mind with God. Eli reacts as a man who naturally gravitates toward structure, toward the ritual 'rules' with which he is familiar and comfortable."[1]

Hannah went beyond inventing a new way of communicating with God, one that would become the template for both private, intimate prayer and formal spoken liturgical practices in Jewish and Christian traditions. She also fashioned a protocol for asking God for what one needs. By requesting what she needed and then promising to reciprocate God's gift, Hannah teaches us that when God answers our prayers, we need to keep God's gift of favor and generosity flowing.

This is what Hannah did when she delivered her precious son to the priests and left him in their hands so that he could serve God. We shouldn't read this too literally. Hannah didn't give her son back to the temple the way one returns a book to the library. She gave Samuel back by raising him to honor and serve God in exemplary ways. Hannah teaches that when we pray to God for good things—such as love or children or good health—and are fortunate enough to receive what we have prayed for, we must give back. We do so by registering our gratitude and by making conscious, constructive plans to translate the gifts we have received into gifts for others.

We begin our own giving back the moment we witness that God is present in the gift. The spirit of the divine giver is in the gift, as the anthropologist Marcel Mauss has written. So the gift is never fully ours in the first place. It's on a long-term loan and our task is to take good care of the gift we appear to possess and share that gift with others.

If the gift we have prayed for and received is a fine home, we can promise to transform our home into a gift for others by making that home into a place where guests feel cared for, welcome, and safe. If the gift is wealth, we can promise to put that wealth to work for others, not only by giving to charity but also by actively stewarding the monies we give away so that good works get done. If the gift is children, we can raise them to be people who will love their siblings, their grandparents, and their pets and eventually, the friends and lovers who will reach out to them. We can teach them that reciprocation isn't always direct. For instance, while we can never fully repay our parents for what they have done for us, we can reciprocate indirectly through the way we care for our children, who, in turn, will reciprocate through their own parenting.

We may find that the answer to our prayers comes when we start to formulate the way we will express our gratitude. This was my experience long ago. The summer before my senior year in high school I went on a study trip to Israel. At the end of the program, we were taken to Yad Vashem, the Holocaust memorial museum in Jerusalem. Heads of state are always taken there, and so is every tour group. The experience one has there is predictable, but not trite. Like other Holocaust memorials, Yad Vashem is the kind of place that leaves you horrified but makes you tender, too, and focuses your resolve to remember the evil of the Holocaust, to bear witness to the lives of those who were killed, and to champion the forces of good. You vow to recognize evil and to keep sight of the preciousness of every moment of your own life—the big ones and the prosaic.

In one of the last halls I walked through, one displaying the photographs of young people and children killed by the Nazis, I was riveted by the picture of a teenage girl who came from the same place as one of my grandparents. Dark frizzy hair, high cheekbones, Eskimo eyes. It was uncanny: she looked so much like me she could have been my sister. I stopped so long people had to go around me.

My thoughts that summer day were hardly original. Had my grandparents not already emigrated to America before the war, they would have surely perished. And I would never have been born. What else could a person conclude but to vow to lead a life worthy of having been spared?

I felt as if the girl in the picture were looking back at me and claiming my soul. I wanted to remember the face of my soul mate for the rest of my life and keep my commitment to a life of moral purpose. Still, however much an idealistic teenager I was, I was realistic about my own enthusiasms. I knew that no matter how strong my feelings were at that moment, the details of everyday life were derailing and I would surely forget.

To fight against forgetfulness, I engaged silently in a Hannah-style negotiation with God, making a request together with a promise.

"Please, God," I prayed, "if you will help me to remember my soul mate always, bearing witness to the evil that claimed her life, and if you help me to live a worthy life, then whatever joy I experience in my life will be half hers. On my graduation day, I will share half the learning; on my wedding day, I will stand in my wedding gown with her and share half the love of my groom; if I carry a baby, it will be half hers to bear; if I have children, they will be half her children to love as well."

I admit, the cerebral exercise of dividing my joy in half and sharing it with a remembered face in a photograph is not generosity as it is usually understood. Even giving up just a teaspoon of chocolate mousse to a dining partner who negotiates for a taste is an act of greater bounteousness.

But the practice of "halving" has become part of my spiritual discipline, an act of awareness to keep in mind. By keeping my end of the promise, my prayer that I live in constant awareness of the lives lost in the Holocaust continues to be answered. When my daughter marched up for her high school diploma, I remembered, "Half of this pride is for you," and when I will celebrate my thirtieth wedding anniversary this summer, I know I will remember, "Half of this enduring love is yours."

This, then, is Hannah's teaching: when we honor the promises we have made to God, we create the possibility that our prayers will be answered.

Embracing the Gift of Hannah

Like Hannah, have the courage to call out to the source of abundance and possibility and pray for what you yourself need: love, friendship, children, health, meaningful work, protection, shelter, more hope and less despair, enough strength to reach tomorrow. Forget that you were once told that it was rude to pray for a bicycle. Why not pray for a wonderful red bicycle that will take you flying down your street when you are seven years old? For many of us, the desire to pray was stolen from us by those who told us we were wickedly selfish if we prayed for our heart's desire and not for world peace.

When you think your own needs are too small and unimportant to bring to God's attention, you stop the conversation. Go ahead and pray for a job that uses your talents, for a passing grade in organic chemistry so you can become a doctor, for a partner who sees your quirks as loveable assets. Understand why you need what you do and explain it, using words or feelings. Permit yourself to feel your prayer being heard, to sense the compassion of divine listening. Like Hannah, you needn't voice your prayers aloud. You can whisper. You can pray in your heart. Pray as you will, where you will. You needn't be bound by any of the conventions legislating the "correctness" of prayer.

Then, anticipating your prayer will be answered, plan ahead, like Hannah, making a commitment as to how you will give back in gratitude for what you hope you may receive. Hannah tells us it is not reprehensible to strike a good bargain with God—it is simply good, holy business.

Trust that you will recognize how your prayer has been answered, knowing that what you request and what you receive may not quite match in the short run. Most importantly, immediately discover ways to keep your end of the bargain.

CHAPTER 18

WOMEN WHO BAKE CAKES FOR THE QUEEN OF HEAVEN
WORSHIPPING AS WOMEN

The Biblical Story

"Hear the word of God," said Jeremiah. . . . "Don't you see what they are doing in the towns of Judah and in the streets of Jerusalem? The children gather the sticks, the fathers build the fire, and the mothers knead the dough to make cakes for the Queen of Heaven. . . ."

A large gathering of women who were present answered Jeremiah's rebuke: "Although you say you speak to us about this matter in the name of the Lord, we will not listen to what you have to say. On the contrary, we will do everything that we have vowed—to make offerings to the Queen of Heaven and to pour libations to her, as we used to do, we and our fathers, our kings, and our officials, in the towns of Judah and the streets of Jerusalem. Because in those days, we had plenty to eat, we were well off, and suffered no misfortune. Ever since we stopped making offerings to the Queen of Heaven and pouring libations to her, we have lacked everything and have been consumed by the sword and by famine. And do you think that when we make offerings to the Queen of Heaven and pour libations to her, it is without our husbands' approval that we have made cakes in her likeness and poured libations to her?"

—Adapted from Jeremiah 7:18; 44:16–19

The Women Who Bake Cakes for the Queen of Heaven's Own Story

The women who bake cakes for the Queen of Heaven were surprised that long after they were forbidden to make their cakes, they could still remember precisely what making them felt like. The experience was richer and deeper than any other memory that sustained them in the dark years of exile. They no longer had their molds, having been forced to give them up when they departed from Judah. But even without the molds to hold on to, without the feel of dough in their hands, the smell of the rising yeast, or the sooty ashes rising up their arms, they could still reconstruct all the feelings of making those wonderful cakes and what it felt like to rush them over to the altar. They remembered that baking was a prayer.

They needed just one thing to jog their memories: the recipe. No one woman could remember all of it, but each woman recalled part. There had never been a single recipe—each woman's mother had her own way. Some mothers used secret ingredients that they wouldn't even say aloud to their own daughters. They would only demonstrate, with a wink or a gesture: two threads of saffron, and not three; the almondy pit of a peach, but just a smidgen, crushed; the rind of a citron, including a few bits of the bitter pith. Now the secrets were out and were passed around like morsels of gossip. When you shared with the others the ingredients you remembered, you felt transported back home, to the place where you belonged, where you felt safe and most fully yourself.

You could even convince yourself that one day you would return home, and you could send the children out to all the old familiar places to gather sticks. The men would fire up the ovens again, each one looking over his shoulder to see how big his neighbor's fire was and feeling smug about the heat of the fire he had made. And you would meet your women friends on the road, and you would complain about how much work it all was: your arms were sore from all the stirring; no one really appreciated all you had done; everyone was complaining about all the work when you were the one who had worked her fingers to the bone. But you would be glowing, because you had loved it all from start to finish and would do it again in an instant.

It was not hard to explain to the men just how you felt. The men had long before taken to sharing their fathers' recipes for holy breads that were grain gifts to God. They made up songs about the recipes so they could remember them. This is the one they chanted about the offerings that old father Aaron and his sons used to make in the holy temple:

> *God spoke to Moses saying,*
> *This is the coming-close offering that Aaron and his sons must bring*
> *   to God:*
> *A tenth of an ephah of choice flour as a grain offering,*
> *Half of it in the morning,*
> *Half of it in the evening,*
> *Prepare it with oil on a griddle.*
> *Stir it well,*
> *And bring it near as baked, crumbled bits of grain,*
> *It will be a pleasing and soothing fragrance for God.*

The men sang, and the women sang with them, and they all remembered. The women knew that however rich their own memories were of making cakes for the Queen of Heaven, unless they created a song their granddaughters could sing for the generations, the recipe—and maybe the Queen of Heaven as well—would be forgotten.

The Women Who Bake Cakes for the Queen of Heaven Speak to Us

As we grow in wisdom, we come to recognize and respect the beauty, holiness, and power there is in religious paths that are different from our own. We come to understand that as much as we believe our own practices are right for us, there are different paths to God.

In ancient Israel, worship of one god was one of the available means of sacred practice. While monotheistic practices have endured, they did not eclipse all other available forms of devotion overnight. Like most new religious practices, monotheism developed and gained predominance over time. Early on, monotheism was expressed in worship through elaborate, precisely designated sacrifices brought by individuals and families and offered up by the temple priests in a central temple. This way of worshipping the one God, through sacrifice, no longer exists for Jews: prayer has replaced it.

From the Bible, we know ancient Israelite women worshipped in different ways even as monotheism was gaining a stronghold. Women in sixth century Judah and Israel worshipped a goddess called the Queen of Heaven and baked cakes to honor her. Husbands, children, and even courtiers became involved in the practice. As long as it lasted, this must have empowered women, helping them to achieve positions of spiritual leadership in both their families and their communities.

We derive the little that we do know about the women who worshipped the Queen of Heaven mostly from the Book of Jeremiah. (Not surprisingly, the Bible tells us much more about the Levite men who made pancakes.) Scholar Susan Ackerman supposes that the Queen of Heaven may have been the Semitic goddesses Ishtar or Astarte, or some amalgam of the two. She was associated with women's fertility, prosperity, and war as well. Her worshippers may have prepared cakes in their own homes, molded in her image, and then baked them in ashes. This was the practice of nearby Mesopotamian women observing the cult of Tammuz, who baked cakes in molds resembling Ishtar. Archaeologists have discovered molds of "a nude female figure who holds her hands cupped under her breasts. Her hips are large and prominent."[1]

The fertility god Tammuz represented springtime and its harvest of firstfruits and newborn calves and lambs. When spring was over, it was as if Tammuz had died, and his lover, Ishtar, who baked cakes as offerings, mourned him.

Information about the practice comes mostly through the prophet Jeremiah's critique of it. He claimed the people of Judah were exiled to Babylonia because God was offended by the sacrifices they—the women in particular—made to other gods.

Women putting their baking skills into divine service? The very thought must have made Jeremiah anxious. It was one thing if women baked for guests (as Sarah did for the angels who visited her and Abraham) or if the male Levite priests baked offerings for God in the Holy Temple following a set of ancient rules. But it was another thing altogether if women themselves were the ritual experts, baking and offering sacrificial cakes to a divinity, following practices passed on orally from mother to daughter.[2] When women bakers brought the cakes they made in their homes to the sacred altars, they achieved more agency than their culture could tolerate. Putting a halt to their practice cut off "women's public access to the divinity and the connection between the private domain of the home and the public arena of ritual."[3]

The women rejected Jeremiah's explanation for God's wrath, rebuffing his condemnation with a ready riposte: "We'll tell you why we now lack everything and suffer from violence and famine. Not because we worshipped the Queen of Heaven, making her offerings, pouring her libations, and burning incense. When we did, we had plenty to eat and were well-off and suffered no misfortune. Our mistake was allowing you to make us stop worshipping the Queen of Heaven."

We can still hear the faint voices of our ancestral mothers. They advise us: "Remember that women have always known many wise ways to embrace the sacred in their lives. And in particular, remember that making food can be holy."

In every faith tradition, food is a powerful conduit to the holy and an expression of being blessed. And who makes the household food—the Easter hams, the Passover matzoh ball soup? Usually the women. Think of all the grandmothers and mothers cooking up holiness for the holidays. What is that crazy cooking, which we may do too, all about? It's about making holy time palpable. It's about the smells and tastes that make a home into a holy place. It's about experiencing belief throughout your body. Through chopping, mixing, kneading, and feeding, it's about loving and being loved. Or, expressed more formally by scholar Susan Sered, who has written extensively on women as ritual experts, "Women have developed ways for religion to sacralize female experience."[4]

In the seventeenth century, women said this blessing before putting their bread into the oven:

Lord of all the world, in your hand is all blessing. I come now to revere your holiness, and I pray you to bestow your blessing on the baked goods. Send an angel to guard the baking, so that all will be well baked, will rise nicely, and will not burn . . . as you blessed the dough of Sarah and Rebecca and our mothers. My Lord God, listen to my voice; you are the God who hears the voices of those who call upon you wholeheartedly.[5]

And at a tent revival meeting that took place one summer in Bedford-Stuyvesant, Brooklyn, the preacher, Sister Brenda Winakur, handed out angel cake to the faithful who had come for healing and blessings. Winakur, quoted in the *New York Times*, explained that the cakes are a "visual representation of Christ, 'just a little point of contact,' . . . to make it easier to connect." At the end of the worship service, the faithful "lined up for their own pieces of cake, in a ritual reminiscent of communion but far more energetic. She put the cake in their open mouths, placed a hand on some of their foreheads. 'Somebody has received the Lord tonight,' she said."[6]

The women who bake cakes remind us to pass on our own wise ways—not just food practices, but all the distinctive ways women bring holiness into life. Don't assume your heirs will know how you brought the sacred into your own life and into theirs. Teach them, and teach them yet again and help them to practice until they, too, know how to make holiness palpable. If you have children, they might remind you of rituals you perform with them that you take for granted, such as braiding a child's hair when she feels sad or placing a welcome-home sign on the door when grown children visit.

How upsetting it must have been when Jeremiah forbade the women from a practice that so deeply sustained them. I asked my friend Molly Bosscher Davis, a mother of two sons, now preparing for ordination as a minister, how she might have reacted if a beloved, central form of worship that was food-centered were banned. Her response was intriguing:

> I can't help but think here of Eucharist—how the Christian consumes God in the ritual and how not having Eucharist leaves one weak and hungry. St. Katherine Drexel, the second American to be canonized, founded an order, the Sisters of the Blessed Sacrament, that had Eucharist every day; this was the center of their self-understanding. The offerings of these women in Jeremiah give them self-understanding and identity. Baking their cakes for the Queen of Heaven is so important that they cannot give it up, even when a prophet of God asks them to. They continue to offer cakes even in the shadow of the threat of doom, which Jeremiah prophesies. There are rituals that I myself would not give up, even if threatened with punishment as well. Eucharist is central for me. And I imagine the Shabbat would be the same for a Jew.

These are the rituals that give a center, an identity that cannot be easily shaken.

Learning about our women ancestors who worshipped a goddess doesn't mean we plan to replicate what they did. Studying their ways, however, does help us make our own rituals more women-centered. Wendy Hunter Roberts, a ritualist and author, who attempted to rediscover recipes for Queen of Heaven cakes (barley, honey, raisin, figs, coriander, wild yeast, safflower oil, and goat curd in crescent-moon-shaped forms), did so in order that women of various traditions would have a way to come together for mutual empowerment and "affirm their own mothers and the Mother of all of us."[7]

The women who baked cakes demonstrate how important it is to hold on to the joy of sacred observances that take place in the context of family. I asked Molly how the women who baked cakes for the Queen of Heaven inspire her. She told me she was moved by the idyllic image of children gathering sticks, fathers stoking the fires, and mothers kneading dough:

> *The whole family participates in the worship as one entity. It seems like you could add "gladly" or "with joy" after each of the tasks performed for the Queen of Heaven. The children gather sticks with joy, the fathers build the fire with joy, etc. This kind of communal activity creates joy and purpose for a family, a sense of identity that helps transcend difficulties. It reminds me of how I'd ideally like our house to run. For example, our sons, Asher and Isak, can set the table and clean up after the meal, my husband, Creston, can cook, and I can do miscellaneous things in the house that need doing, or vice versa. This is sometimes how it works, but our house is not always the vision of organic helping. One person is tired, another is gone, the boys want to ride their bikes after dinner, or we have guests.*

Molly is also moved by the hands-on participation in worship:

> *While our family loves church, there is no sense in which we "get our hands dirty" or participate in the worship like these families seem to. We don't have to gather wood for the fire or bake cakes for worship.*

Our Eucharist is a mass-produced unleavened wafer, which the Altar Guild buys from a church catalogue. I know that in the Eastern Orthodox Church things are different. Author Fredrica Mathewes-Green has described how the job of baking the Eucharist bread shifts between different families in her church. She also tells how she loves some of the breads more than others. We went to a church for a while where the bread was baked by a woman in the congregation. It was fabulous, sweet and pita-like (perhaps like the cakes?).

The women who bake cakes for the Queen of Heaven bid us to honor their memory as we recall their practices and other women's sacred practices throughout history that have been criticized, forgotten, or suppressed.

They bid us, as well, to note those aspects of our own lives and our own yearning that are not well-represented in the kinds of worship that are now available to us. Do our rituals connect us to nature, helping us to observe the cyclical changes in seasons and celebrate the particular blessings each season brings? Do they connect us to the earth, helping us to tend it and be grateful for its yield? Do they remind us that each of us can, in our own kitchen, create a humble and lovely cake?

The women who bake cakes for the Queen of Heaven challenge us to be sure that the rituals of our lives reflect us. They encourage us to hold on to rituals that express our agency, power, and distinctive connections to the sacred. Where such rituals are lacking, we must, with wisdom and with loving ties to the traditions we have inherited, create them.

Embracing the Gift of the Women Who Bake Cakes for the Queen of Heaven

While you may be ready to get out your mixing bowl and start kneading a dough of barley, figs, and coriander and shaping it into crescent cakes, the women who bake cakes for the Queen of Heaven have a different practice in mind. Theirs is a ritual of reflection and discernment. The women who bake cakes for the Queen of Heaven ask us to dwell on the rituals and practices that move us and hold our lives together most.

In doing so, we can acknowledge that in our own lives, some inherited rituals that are performed by women work well, while others have less meaning for us, no matter how many times we've tried to perform them. Why is this so? I suspect, in part, it's because so many of our inherited rituals have been designed and maintained by men and for men. Why should they happen to work for women? This has clear analogies in medicine, where it took a long time for doctors to acknowledge that drugs or procedures tested only in men don't always act the same way in women's bodies. It has analogies in the U.S. military, too. With more women soldiers serving than ever before, military experts are just now realizing that practices and regulations that have worked for men do not always work for women. Consider the military jumpsuit, for instance: it works for the male soldier fighting to climb out of his tank and unzip his suit to take a quick pee, but for the female soldier, the regulation jumpsuit is a source of embarrassment and is even potentially life-threatening. She has to find a place private enough to take off her whole jumpsuit! Yes—and I don't think I am revealing a top secret, because I read this in a magazine in the dentist's office—a new women-friendly jumpsuit with a drop-seat is being designed.

How can we measure the efficacy of rituals for women? It's complicated, because we're wise enough not to judge any ritual by its working in too literal a way. That is, we know not to measure the efficacy of healing prayers by the number of times a sick person we've been praying for has gotten well. If it's a prayer for peace, we know not to check off "Success!" only when we hear there's a cease-fire or the troops are sent home.

Instead, we ask if the ritual has meaning and power. To examine the rituals you regularly perform, start by listing them over the course of a week. These could be religious rituals or rituals that get you through the week—such as having a family dinner together, performing Sunday chores, or doing elaborate bedtime rituals with a child, involving a bath, stories, and songs. They could be rituals that bring people together to commemorate important events or memories, or they could be ones that comfort, heal, teach, or move us along through life's passages.

When you've got your list, glance at this group of traits that effective rituals tend to have. It was compiled by Meg Cox, author of *The*

Heart of a Family and *The Book of New Family Traditions*, who has studied family rituals. Effective rituals:

- Impart a sense of identity
- Provide comfort and security
- Help us to navigate change
- Teach values
- Cultivate knowledge of cultural or religious heritage
- Teach practical skills
- Solve problems
- Keep alive a sense of departed family members
- Create wonderful memories
- Generate joy[8]

How many of these traits do your own rituals have? You're likely to see that your most effective rituals are the ones that meet a good many of the criteria.

You may discover, as I did, that some of your best rituals are conventional practices you have modified to better reflect a woman's life. Take our unconventional Sabbath practice. It started years ago when my children were small and my husband was a college chaplain. Along with the students we had invited as guests, we had to race through our Sabbath meal in order to get to services at the college. When my husband's vacations came around, I wanted to celebrate my not having to rush through a dinner with company and dash out. I wanted to recognize that after working, caring for kids, and preparing for the Sabbath, I was exhausted. So when the Sabbath fell during vacation, I would bathe the kids, and then we would all get dressed—not in our Sabbath best, as we usually did, but in our pajamas. It symbolized the pleasure we took in being able to stay home and have a leisurely family dinner alone. Even now, whenever we are together as a family for Sabbath and don't have company coming, we have our dinner in our pajamas. (We have special Sabbath pj's: they're the ones with tops and bottoms that more or less match.) The ritual works for us all, because it celebrates our identity and history as a family and increases the joy of our Sabbath observance.

I have another ritual to mark renewal. It began when a group of young women clergy, students of mine, asked if I would join them to prepare for the New Year. I was touched that they asked me, and imagined they'd be doing something very spiritual, such as silent meditation, studying about renewal and repentance, or taking a ritual bath. I said, "Count me in," and took down the assigned time—noon—and a meeting place on 33rd Street in New York, which I figured must be a meditation center.

When I arrived, I thought I had taken down the wrong address, because I ended up at a nail salon. Momentarily, my students came walking down the street. I wasn't mistaken. They had made appointments for us all to have manicures and pedicures! It made total sense for them: they were going to be officiating in the coming days. Perhaps they envied their congregants, who could mark the New Year by wearing new clothes, while they, having to wear clerical robes, missed the excuse to buy a new holiday outfit. But with gussied-up fingers and toes, they too could wear signs of renewal! I wasn't bold enough to have a pedicure that day, but I did have my first manicure. Since then, I get a manicure whenever I want to mark a new beginning. I also get one when I feel I am getting too serious. I know I will be sure to laugh when I remember the row of my otherwise so-serious, sensible, and bespectacled clergy women, each with one foot soaking in a plastic tub of sudsy water and the other foot in a flip-flop, her toes separated by cotton balls. Were I to go through a major change in my life and needed to do something "extra-strength," I suppose I could spring for the pedicure.

Finally, there's my approach to institutionalized worship, which has little to do with reciting the mandatory liturgy. You may find this familiar. When I go to a house of worship, my mouth might be saying the prayers, but my deeper prayer is observing people I have come to pray with, and celebrating the gift of being part of a community. I might see the families that brought us dinners when we were sick and the family we gathered toys for when their house burned down. I used to see the teenagers who babysat for my daughters; now I see the kids my own daughters once babysat for becoming teenagers. I see the people we've all been praying for, and I'll send a smile toward the family that finally located a bone-marrow donor for their fourteen-year-old daughter after the whole congregation showed up to get tested. Recognizing how deeply we are caught up in each other's stories is what makes public worship so spiritually fulfilling for me.

Once you've designated the rituals or practices that work best for you, honor the women who bake cakes for the Queen of Heaven and honor yourself by passing those best practices on to family members, students, or friends who will appreciate that you are giving them a treasured gift.

AFTERWORD
AN INVITATION

But what about all the other women of the Bible?, you may well ask. The ones we know by name, such as Rachel, Zipporah, Deborah, Yael, Delilah, and the witch of Endor? What about all the other biblical women we know as types, such as the midwives; the virgins; the newly married women; or the daughters of Zion who, in Lamentations, "pour out their hearts like water"?

There are so many more women to encounter, so much wisdom to uncover and take to heart. It is my hope that in reading *Sarah Laughed* and in performing your version of some of the rituals, you might come to experience women of the Bible as I have, as real people who are intimate, endearingly familiar, and wise. Alone, or with people with whom you can read deeply, why not invite the many other women of the Bible into your own life? Hear their stories, attend to their wisdom. Let them be the sources of inspiration that they are.

In my own experience, the women of the Bible traveled farther than halfway to meet me. For you, I trust they will do the same, if, with care and patience, you allow them to.

ACKNOWLEDGMENTS

For the vision behind this work, thanks go to Lynn Rosen, and for the encouragement to produce it, I thank Judith McCarthy and her colleagues at McGraw-Hill, especially Katherine Hinkebein and Mandy Huber. I thank the Center for Study of Religion at Princeton University, where I was a visiting fellow during part of the time I was writing this book, and I thank Ze'eva Cohen, who invited me to dance my way into the Bible.

I thank the good women who made all the difference, each in her own way: Juliana Ochs, Elizabeth Ochs, Susan Grandis Goldstein, Evelyn Polesny, Lauren Winner, Alice Nakhimovsky, Margaret Mohrman, Deborah Healy, Amy Kaplan, Phyllis Leffler, Anne Kinney, Jan Dorman, Rose Capon, Dela Alexander, Karen Marsh, Rachel Cousineau, Channa Meyer, Elizabeth Shanks Alexander, Rachel Sabath-Beit Halachmi, Dianne Cohler-Esses, Molly Bosscher Davis, Judith Kovacs, Vicky Bravo, Dahlia Lithwick, Eleni Zatz Litt, Sandy Sussman, Ayala Shiffman, Riv-Ellen Prell, Rene Levine Melamed, Tsili Reisenberger, and my University of Virginia students.

Finally, I thank Peter Ochs, because . . . that's what we do.

NOTES

Introduction

1. Judith Plaskow, *Standing Again at Sinai: Judaism from a Feminist Perspective* (San Francisco: Harper San Francisco, 1991), p. 55.
2. Kathleen Norris, *Dakota: Spiritual Geography* (New York: Tickner and Fields, 1993).
3. Judith Plaskow, "Jewish Memory from a Feminist Perspective" in *Weaving the Visions: New Patterns in Feminist Spirituality*, eds. Judith Plaskow and Carol Christ (New York: Harper and Row, 1986), p. 46.

Chapter 1 Eve: Tasting Wisdom

1. Martin Buber, *On the Bible: Eighteen Studies*, ed. Nahum Glatzer (New York: Schocken Books, 1982), p. 16.
2. Mary F. Belenky, Blythe M. Clinchy, Nancy R. Goldberger, and Jill M. Tarule, *Women's Ways of Knowing: The Development of Self, Voice, and Mind* (New York: Basic Books, 1986), p. 3.

Chapter 4 The Daughters of Tzlofhad: Speaking Out in a Man's World

1. Judith Baskin, *Midrashic Women: Formations of the Feminine in Rabbinic Literature* (Hanover and London: Brandeis University Press, 1997), p. 144.

2. Baskin, p. 145.

3. My friend since childhood, Naamah Kelman, who became the first woman to be educated and ordained as a Reform rabbi in Israel, first pointed this out to me.

4. Gloria Steinem, "Women and Leadership," in *Lifecycles*, ed. D. Orenstein and J. Litman (Woodstock, VT: Jewish Lights Publishing, 1997), p. 302.

Chapter 5   The Woman of Valor: Repairing the World in Your Own Way

1. This lovely translation is by Saul Zipkin and appears in *Eit Hazamir Higiya*, a book of songs and blessings that he and his wife created for their wedding and has since been reproduced (dzik@aya.yale.edu). Used with permission.

2. E. M. Broner, *Bringing Home the Light: A Jewish Woman's Handbook of Rituals* (San Francisco: Council Oak Books, 1999), p. 73–74.

Chapter 8   Jephthah's Daughter: Being There for Friends

1. Lauren Slater, *Welcome to My Country* (New York: Anchor, 1997), p. xiii.

2. Slater, *Welcome to My Country*, p. xiii.

Chapter 10   Sarah: Protecting Your Dreams

1. Allegra Goodman, "Sarah," in *The Family Markowitz* (New York: Washington Square Press, 1996), p. 231.

2. September 7, 2003, "The Futile Pursuit of Happiness."

Chapter 12   Yocheved: Letting Children Go

1. Martin Buber, *Tales of the Hasidim: The Early Masters* (New York: Schocken Books, 1947, 1979), p. 42.

2. Gina Bria, "Celebrating Kinship with Family Rituals," *New York Times*, July 13, 1995.

3. *Prayers for a Thousand Years*, ed. Elizabeth Roberts and Elias Amidon (San Francisco: Harper San Francisco, 1999), p. 166.

Chapter 13 The Woman Who Has Given Birth

1. This quote is from a work-in-progress by Dianne Cohler-Esses on the experience of childbirth. Used with permission.
2. Ibid.
3. Robert F. Murphy, *The Body Silent: The Different World of the Disabled* (New York: W. W. Norton, 1990).

Chapter 14 Job's Wife: Healing by Expressing Anger

1. Melissa Weintraub, "The Uses and Dangers of Numbness," *Forward*, January 2, 2004.
2. Ilana Pardes, *Countertraditions in the Bible: A Feminist Approach* (Cambridge: Harvard University Press, 1992), p. 147–148.
3. *The Jewish Week*, June 14, 2002.
4. Howard W. French, "Japan's Neglected Resources: Female Workers," *New York Times*, July 24, 2003.
5. Pardes, *Countertraditions*, p. 149.
6. Harold Kushner, *When Bad Things Happen to Good People* (New York: Avon Books, 1983), p. 45.

Chapter 15 Vashti: Taking Care of Yourself

1. Erica Goode, "Study Says 20% of Girls Reported Abuse by a Date," *New York Times*, August 1, 2001, p. A10.

Chapter 17 Hannah: Seeking God

1. Leila Gul Berner, "Hearing Hannah's Voice: The Jewish Feminist Challenge and Ritual Innovation," in *Daughters of Abraham: Feminist Thought in Judaism, Christianity, and Islam*, ed. Yvonne Haddad and John Esposito (Gainesville: University Press of Florida, 2002), p. 38.

Chapter 18 Women Who Bake Cakes for the Queen of Heaven: Worshipping as Women

1. Susan Ackerman, "'And the Women Knead Dough': The Worship of the Queen of Heaven in Sixth-Century Judah," in

Gender and Difference in Ancient Israel, ed. Peggy L. Day (Minneapolis: Fortress Press, 1989), p. 115.

2. See Nina Mandel, "Spirituality, Baking, and the Queen of Heaven," *Nashim*, no. 5 (Fall 2002), p. 46.

3. Mandel, p. 49.

4. Susan Sered, *Women as Ritual Experts: The Religious Lives of Elderly Jewish Women in Jerusalem* (Oxford: Oxford University Press, 1992), p. 4.

5. Translated by Chava Weissler in *Voices of the Matriarchs: Listening to the Prayers of Early Modern Jewish Women* (Boston: Beacon Press, 1998), p. ix.

6. Diane Cardwell, "Yes, a Tent Revival. Yes, in Brooklyn." *New York Times*, August 12, 2003.

7. Wendy Hunter Roberts, *Celebrating Her: Feminist Ritualizing Comes of Age* (Cleveland: Pilgrim Press, 1998), p. 10–11.

8. Meg Cox, *The Heart of a Family: Searching America for New Traditions That Fulfill Us* (New York: Random House, 1998), p. 16.

INDEX